OPPOSING VIEWPOINTS® SERIES

Homelessness

Other Books of Related Interest:

Opposing Viewpoints Series

Chemical Dependency

Child Custody

Domestic Violence

Juvenile Crime

Poverty

Street Teens

At Issue Series

Alcohol Abuse

Alternatives to Prisons

Do Veterans Receive Adequate Health Care?

How Can the Poor Be Helped?

Current Controversies Series

The Elderly

Illegal Immigration

Jobs in America

The Uninsured

"Congress shall make no law . . . abridging the freedom of speech, or of the press."

First Amendment to the US Constitution

The basic foundation of our democracy is the First Amendment guarantee of freedom of expression. The Opposing Viewpoints series is dedicated to the concept of this basic freedom and the idea that it is more important to practice it than to enshrine it.

OPPOSING VIEWPOINTS® SERIES

Homelessness

Tamara Thompson, Book Editor

GREENHAVEN PRESS
A part of Gale, Cengage Learning

GALE
CENGAGE Learning·

Detroit • New York • San Francisco • New Haven, Conn • Waterville, Maine • London

Elizabeth Des Chenes, *Managing Editor*

© 2012 Greenhaven Press, a part of Gale, Cengage Learning.

Gale and Greenhaven Press are registered trademarks used herein under license.

For more information, contact:
Greenhaven Press
27500 Drake Rd.
Farmington Hills, MI 48331-3535
Or you can visit our Internet site at gale.cengage.com

For product information and technology assistance, contact us at

Gale Customer Support, 1-800-877-4253
For permission to use material from this text or product, submit all requests online at
www.cengage.com/permissions

Further permissions questions can be emailed to permissionrequest@cengage.com

Articles in Greenhaven Press anthologies are often edited for length to meet page requirements. In addition, original titles of these works are changed to clearly present the main thesis and to explicitly indicate the author's opinion. Every effort is made to ensure that Greenhaven Press accurately reflects the original intent of the authors. Every effort has been made to trace the owners of copyrighted material.

Cover Image copyright © Ocean/Corbis.

LIBRARY OF CONGRESS CATALOGING-IN-PUBLICATION DATA

Homelessness / Tamara Thompson, book editor.
    p. cm. -- (Opposing viewpoints)
    Includes bibliographical references and index.
    ISBN 978-0-7377-5939-6 (hbk.) -- ISBN 978-0-7377-5940-2 (pbk.)
    1. Homelessness--United States. 2. Homeless persons--United States. I. Thompson, Tamara.
    HV4505.H65528 2012
    362.5'920973--dc23

                                            2011047011

Printed in the United States of America
1 2 3 4 5 6 7 16 15 14 13 12

Contents

Chapter 3: What Housing Policies Will Benefit the Homeless?

Chapter 4: What Policies Will Reduce Homelessness?

Why Consider Opposing Viewpoints?

> "The only way in which a human being can make some approach to knowing the whole of a subject is by hearing what can be said about it by persons of every variety of opinion and studying all modes in which it can be looked at by every character of mind. No wise man ever acquired his wisdom in any mode but this."
>
> *John Stuart Mill*

In our media-intensive culture it is not difficult to find differing opinions. Thousands of newspapers and magazines and dozens of radio and television talk shows resound with differing points of view. The difficulty lies in deciding which opinion to agree with and which "experts" seem the most credible. The more inundated we become with differing opinions and claims, the more essential it is to hone critical reading and thinking skills to evaluate these ideas. Opposing Viewpoints books address this problem directly by presenting stimulating debates that can be used to enhance and teach these skills. The varied opinions contained in each book examine many different aspects of a single issue. While examining these conveniently edited opposing views, readers can develop critical thinking skills such as the ability to compare and contrast authors' credibility, facts, argumentation styles, use of persuasive techniques, and other stylistic tools. In short, the Opposing Viewpoints Series is an ideal way to attain the higher-level thinking and reading skills so essential in a culture of diverse and contradictory opinions.

In addition to providing a tool for critical thinking, Opposing Viewpoints books challenge readers to question their own strongly held opinions and assumptions. Most people form their opinions on the basis of upbringing, peer pressure, and personal, cultural, or professional bias. By reading carefully balanced opposing views, readers must directly confront new ideas as well as the opinions of those with whom they disagree. This is not to argue simplistically that everyone who reads opposing views will—or should—change his or her opinion. Instead, the series enhances readers' understanding of their own views by encouraging confrontation with opposing ideas. Careful examination of others' views can lead to the readers' understanding of the logical inconsistencies in their own opinions, perspective on why they hold an opinion, and the consideration of the possibility that their opinion requires further evaluation.

Evaluating Other Opinions

To ensure that this type of examination occurs, Opposing Viewpoints books present all types of opinions. Prominent spokespeople on different sides of each issue as well as well-known professionals from many disciplines challenge the reader. An additional goal of the series is to provide a forum for other, less known, or even unpopular viewpoints. The opinion of an ordinary person who has had to make the decision to cut off life support from a terminally ill relative, for example, may be just as valuable and provide just as much insight as a medical ethicist's professional opinion. The editors have two additional purposes in including these less known views. One, the editors encourage readers to respect others' opinions—even when not enhanced by professional credibility. It is only by reading or listening to and objectively evaluating others' ideas that one can determine whether they are worthy of consideration. Two, the inclusion of such viewpoints encourages the important critical thinking skill of objectively evaluating an author's credentials and bias. This evaluation will illuminate an author's reasons for taking a particular stance on an issue and will aid in readers' evaluation of the author's ideas.

It is our hope that these books will give readers a deeper understanding of the issues debated and an appreciation of the complexity of even seemingly simple issues when good and honest people disagree. This awareness is particularly important in a democratic society such as ours in which people enter into public debate to determine the common good. Those with whom one disagrees should not be regarded as enemies but rather as people whose views deserve careful examination and may shed light on one's own.

Thomas Jefferson once said that "difference of opinion leads to inquiry, and inquiry to truth." Jefferson, a broadly educated man, argued that "if a nation expects to be ignorant and free . . . it expects what never was and never will be." As individuals and as a nation, it is imperative that we consider the opinions of others and examine them with skill and discernment. The Opposing Viewpoints series is intended to help readers achieve this goal.

David L. Bender and Bruno Leone,
Founders

Introduction

> *"Extreme poverty and homelessness are useful abstracts that only dimly reflect the concrete human details of the extremely poor and the homeless."*
>
> —Peter H. Rossi,
> *Down and Out in America:*
> *The Origins of Homelessness*

Homelessness in the United States is not a recent phenomenon, and contrary to popular belief, the problem did not arise in the past few decades with the closure of mental hospitals, the influx of Vietnam veterans, or even the deep cuts to federal housing assistance. Rather, homelessness in America is as old as the country itself, and responses to the problem have not varied much since the beginning—until now.

When colonists first settled in the New World, they brought along English poor laws and Elizabethan attitudes about who was worthy to receive charitable aid. These became the basis for strict settlement laws, under which prospective colonists had to petition city leaders for permission to live in a community. As undesirable individuals and families were refused settlement in town after town, it created a large underclass of poor, homeless wanderers—the country's first homeless population. The attitude that homeless people are unworthy of assistance still persists today, and such views often motivate those who oppose public aid programs.

As the colonies grew, frontier violence and wars (King Philip's War, the French-Indian War, and the American Revolution) caused more homelessness, and by the 1730s, the problem was so prevalent that major cities such as New York and Philadelphia built poorhouses—the first iteration of the city-run emergency shelters that serve homeless people today.

As the Industrial Revolution drew millions from rural areas to cities, a new urban poverty took root and homelessness jumped dramatically; youth homelessness emerged as adolescent boys left home and sought their fortunes. An economic recession in 1853 added to the growing crisis, and the shelter system expanded to include police stations that opened their doors every night to house tens of thousands.

Veterans returning from the Civil War, however, became the first public face of homelessness in America—the iconic train-hopping "tramps" or "hobos" who traveled the country doing transient labor. Public opinion of their drifting lifestyle was harsh, and the aggressive anti-vagrancy laws of this era are the predecessors of contemporary laws that criminalize the activities of homelessness, such as panhandling, sleeping on sidewalks, urinating in public, and other "quality of life" crimes.

When the Great Depression came along in 1929, homelessness skyrocketed nationwide and prompted a large-scale federal response. In 1933, the Federal Emergency Relief Act created the Federal Transient Service, which provided some forty thousand people with shelter, meals, medical care, and job training. After effectively slashing homelessness, the program was dismantled two years later to fund Social Security.

As the country emerged from the Depression and stepped into the rekindled economy of World War II, homelessness leveled out and became concentrated in areas of major cities known as skid rows, where itinerate unskilled laborers could find charitable missions, cheap hotels, day labor offices, secondhand clothing stores, and other basic services. Skid rows remained the status quo for homelessness until the mid 1960s, when such areas—which by then had become quite seedy—were largely wiped out by inner-city renewal projects and urban gentrification.

The homeless ranks swelled again in the 1970s and throughout the '80s as cuts in federal housing assistance, the loss of affordable housing units, the deinstitutionalization of state mental patients, a flood of uprooted and traumatized Vietnam veterans, the growth of substance abuse, and the onset of AIDS (acquired immune deficiency syndrome) converged to increase the risk of homelessness for many groups. This time, because they were no longer centralized in skid row areas, homeless people became much more visible in American cities as they staked out public spots for sleeping or storing their belongings. The public outcry was again harsh, and the official response was often straight from the history books: emergency shelters and other temporary housing; crackdowns on panhandling and other quality-of-life crimes; and partisan squabbles about whether certain types of homeless people— such as those who were able bodied and could work or those who abused substances—were worthy of assistance.

Now, after many years of remaining relatively stable, the number of unsheltered individuals is growing again because of the recent economic recession, rising unemployment, increasing housing costs, and the continuing mortgage foreclosure crisis. According to the National Coalition to End Homelessness's 2009 *State of Homelessness in America* report, the nation's homeless population increased by approximately twenty thousand people from 2008 to 2009 (3 percent). All types of homeless increased, with the biggest jump being for families. According to *Homelessness in America: The Big Picture*, a web seminar presented by the National Center on Family Homelessness and the Center for Social Innovation, "Homelessness has been endemic throughout American history. At times it has become epidemic. Now is one of those times."

Indeed, those who work in social services and government agencies that serve the homeless say that the current crisis is dire; but they also say that despite the numbers, there is a reason for hope. They point to the federal government's first-ever comprehensive plan to address homelessness, *Opening Doors: Federal Strategic Plan to Prevent and End Homelessness*, as a radical new approach that rejects the long-standing view that homelessness is an entrenched problem that cannot be solved. The four key goals of the 2010 plan include the following: 1) Finish the job of ending chronic homelessness in five years; (2) Prevent and end homelessness among veterans in five years; (3) Prevent and end homelessness for families, youth, and children in ten years; and (4) Set a path to ending all types of homelessness.

"While homelessness has grown, our knowledge about what can be done to prevent and end homelessness has also increased," the report states. What the policies and practices promoted by the *Strategic Plan* all have in common are an ambitious commitment to ending homelessness, not just managing it; a growing emphasis on homelessness prevention and outreach; a new reliance on evidence-based practices that promote only the most effective services; the emergence of rapid rehousing and housing-first programs as first-choice interventions; better integration of housing and supportive services; and finally, an increasing awareness about the unique needs of homeless subgroups, such as veterans, children, LGBT (lesbian, gay, bisexual, and transgender) individuals, foster youth, the mentally ill, substance abusers, and victims of domestic violence.

As US Secretary of Housing and Urban Development Shaun Donovan writes in the report's preface, "By working together in new ways, we can—for the first time—set a path to end homelessness for the over 640,000 men, women, and children who are without housing on any single night in our country. They cannot afford to wait."

In *Opposing Viewpoints: Homelessness*, various authors examine the root causes of homelessness and explore proposals for reducing the problem in the following chapters: Is Homelessness a Serious Problem?, What Factors Contribute to Homelessness?, What Housing Policies Will Benefit the Homeless?, and What Policies Will Reduce Homelessness? Throughout these chapters, the authors examine the programs and policies that shape the modern public policy agenda on homelessness.

CHAPTER 1

Is Homelessness a Serious Problem?

Chapter Preface

According to the US Census Bureau, over the next three decades the number of Americans aged sixty-five and older will double to nearly seventy million—more than twice the population of Canada. The force behind such explosive growth is the aging baby boomer generation, the seventy-six million people born between 1946 and 1964. The boomers are the nation's largest demographic group, and the first members of this massive cohort have already entered their fifties; the last will turn fifty-five in 2019. By 2030, roughly 20 percent of the population will be over sixty-five, compared to less than 13 percent in 2011. The number of older people who are homeless is expected to increase proportionally, right along with them.

A 2010 report by the National Alliance to End Homelessness (NAEH) projects a 33 percent increase over the next decade in elderly people who are homeless. The current estimate of 44,172 homeless people over age sixty-two nationwide would jump to 58,772. Such a dramatic demographic shift in the homeless population could have "huge implications" for social service providers and should be seen as a warning that a more extensive safety net of services for seniors will soon be needed, NAEH president Nan Roman told the *Wichita Eagle* newspaper in March 2010. Roman's nonprofit recommends more subsidized housing for the elderly, more permanent housing for all ages, and more research to better assess the needs of the growing population of homeless seniors.

The overall number of seniors (and homeless seniors) will increase as boomers age. In addition, people today live longer than at any time in history, and the number of the oldest old—those over eighty-five—is expected to jump from 4.2 million in 1999 to 19 million by 2050. This is because most people now die from chronic conditions such as cancer, heart trouble, or Alzheimer's disease that progress slowly and require long-term care. Health conditions, medications, and normal age-related declines in vision, cognitive ability, range of motion, and attention span all make elderly homeless people especially vulnerable to life on the street; it also means the health and housing needs of increasing old and frail homeless elders may not be adequately met by the current network of social services.

Pat Hanrahan, president of the United Way of the Plains, told the *Wichita Eagle* that he expects social services organizations will need to change their focus as the population of elderly homeless grows. "The older they get, they're just more fragile and you need a system there to watch for them and take care of them as their physical needs change and their mental needs as well," he said. As the baby boomer generation ages, the country will face major challenges as it responds to the changing needs of this uniquely large group. Those who work with the homeless will be at the forefront of confronting the coming "age wave." The authors in this chapter discuss how various types of individuals are affected by homelessness.

"Nationwide, some 9.6 million families spend more than half of their income on housing, putting them at high risk of becoming homeless."

Homelessness Is a Serious Problem Nationwide

Christine Vestal

In the following viewpoint, Stateline staff writer Christine Vestal maintains that cities nationwide are seeing an unprecedented increase in homelessness due to rising poverty and unemployment and a severe shortage of affordable housing caused by the recent economic recession. Vestal notes that a large percentage of the newly homeless are families with children and that they typically exhaust all their personal resources and housing options before seeking assistance. State and local governments, Vestal maintains, are increasingly hard-pressed to help such individuals because public agencies themselves are strapped for cash just like families are. Vestal points to President Barack Obama's economic stimulus package as offering several forms of relief to help offset the burgeoning homeless crisis. Stateline is a nonpartisan, nonprofit news service of the Pew Center on the States that reports and analyzes trends in state policy nationwide.

As you read, consider the following questions:

1. What does the author regard as "one of the most alarming aspects of the economic crisis"?

2. What do experts agree is the only effective method for reducing homelessness?

3. According to the author, how is this recession's effect on housing different than that of past economic downturns?

Nearly 700 homeless families in Massachusetts are living in hotels at state expense because emergency shelters are full. New York City saw a 40 percent rise in families seeking shelter since the recession began. School districts nationwide reported more homeless kids in the fall of 2008 than the entire year before. And tent cities have sprung up throughout Hawaii and in Sacramento, Calif., Reno, Nev., Phoenix, Portland, Ore., and other cities.

It's one of the most alarming aspects of the economic crisis: State officials are seeing levels of homelessness they have never seen before. President Barack Obama's $787 billion economic stimulus package includes $1.5 billion to address the problem, but officials say it's not enough to cover the cost of housing for millions of families in crisis.

As many as 3.4 million Americans are likely to experience homelessness this year [2009]—a 35 percent increase since the recession started in December 2007—and a majority will be families with children, according to the National Alliance to End Homelessness. The predictions are based on rising levels of unemployment and poverty, plus a severe shortage of affordable housing created, in part, by the mortgage industry collapse.

Families Exhaust Their Options

By the time a family shows up in a shelter, they've done everything possible to avoid homelessness—stayed with friends and family members, gone without food and sold their possessions. They've expended every financial and social resource they have. Some were middle-class families felled by layoffs and ballooning mortgages.

Nationwide, some 9.6 million families spend more than half of their income on housing, putting them at high risk of becoming homeless, according to the National Low Income Housing Coalition. In addition, apartment building foreclosures are causing families to be evicted even when they are paying rent on time, said Linda Couch, the coalition's deputy director.

Before the economic crisis struck, states had made progress getting homeless families and individuals off the street. Homelessness declined 10 percent between 2005 and 2007, as states and cities began subsidizing permanent housing for working families and moving chronically homeless individuals with disabilities into specialized care facilities.

But as homelessness rises, revenue-strapped states will be hard-pressed to maintain those gains.

Experts agree that the only effective method of reducing homelessness is to quickly move people into permanent homes and pay their rent until they regain their footing. Without stable housing, people's lives continue to unravel, no matter how much state support they get. But paying a family's rent is an expensive proposition.

"You need a lot of cash to help these families pay for housing because they're so poor and rents are still very high, and many need a year or more to find jobs," said Robyn Frost, director of the Massachusetts Coalition for the Homeless.

The Stimulus Package Should Help

Obama's stimulus package includes a ninefold immediate increase in an existing grant program that funds shelters. But instead of going to shelters, the funds are dedicated to either helping families hold onto their homes or subsidizing housing for those already homeless.

The Rate of Homelessness

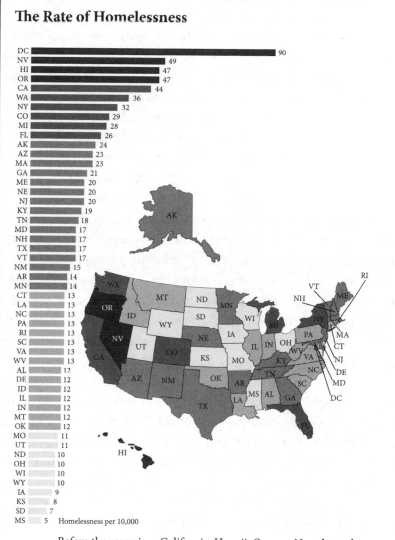

State	Rate
DC	90
NV	49
HI	47
OR	47
CA	44
WA	36
NY	32
CO	29
MI	28
FL	26
AK	24
AZ	23
MA	23
GA	21
ME	20
NE	20
NJ	20
KY	19
TN	18
MD	17
NH	17
TX	17
VT	17
NM	15
AR	14
MN	14
CT	13
LA	13
NC	13
PA	13
RI	13
SC	13
VA	13
WV	13
AL	12
DE	12
ID	12
IL	12
IN	12
MT	12
OK	12
MO	11
UT	11
ND	10
OH	10
WI	10
WY	10
IA	9
KS	8
SD	7
MS	5

Homelessness per 10,000

Before the recession, California, Hawaii, Oregon, Nevada, and Washington State had the highest rates of homelessness. In 2009, homelessness is expected to rise 35 percent nationwide. These data came from the National Alliance to End Homelessness, January 2009.

TAKEN FROM: Christine Vestal, "States Cope with Rising Homelessness," Stateline.org, March 18, 2009. www.stateline.org.

"The emphasis is on prevention, because helping people facing eviction or foreclosure stay in their homes and keeping kids in the schools they're enrolled in will save states money on health care and corrections in the long run," said Michael Stoops, director of the National Coalition for the Homeless.

Before the recession, 41 percent of the homeless population was families with children and most held jobs. About 25 percent—the most visible, chronically homeless—suffered from mental illness or drug addiction. "Now, because of foreclosures and layoffs, we're seeing middle-class families—not just the working poor—in shelters," Stoops said.

In addition to shoring up homelessness prevention programs, advocates for the poor say Congress should have included money for low-income rental assistance, programs they say languished during the [George W.] Bush administration. In economic downturns, rents often get cheaper, making it easier for states to support homeless families. But in this recession, fueled by millions of home foreclosures, the supply of housing has tightened forcing rents to go higher.

"In some parts of the country, rental costs are so high that even if people get their jobs back, they can't afford housing. There are literally millions of people that don't earn enough to afford what the market charges," said Barbara Sard, an analyst with low-income advocacy group the Center on Budget and Policy Priorities.

The Affordable Housing Supply

Although advocates for the poor urged Congress to include low-income rental assistance in the stimulus package, many members were concerned that any expansion of the $40 billion federal housing programs would be difficult to scale back after the stimulus period ended. So instead, states are negotiating with landlords for lower rates and many are trying to purchase and rehabilitate boarded-up homes for low-income families.

Advocates are hopeful that provisions in the stimulus package such as expanded unemployment benefits, food stamps and welfare will help alleviate the homeless crisis. "But until unemployment goes back down, we're going to be up against it. When that gets fixed, things will start getting better," said Steve Berg, director of the National Alliance [to End Homelessness].

The stimulus package includes two other programs that experts say could have a positive long-term effect on the supply of affordable housing: a $4 billion public housing fund for rehabilitating vacant apartments and a $4.2 billion neighborhood stabilization program to help communities purchase foreclosed properties.

But Berg cautioned that the current surge in homelessness will have lasting repercussions.

A new study from the National Center on Family Homelessness, which found that one in 50 American children is homeless, said the disruption and isolation caused by homelessness affects kids the rest of their lives. Children experiencing homelessness have twice the rate of health and emotional problems compared to those with stable housing and they have significantly lower high school graduation rates, the report found.

"*Poverty has been going on for so long and people ignored it, but now it's hitting the middle class, and people are paying attention. We should've been trying to find solutions years ago.*"

Homelessness Is a Growing Problem Among Older and Middle-Class Americans

Carole Fleck

The country's recent economic turmoil and foreclosure crisis have caused a sharp increase in homelessness among older and middle-class Americans, according to the following viewpoint by Carole Fleck, senior editor at the AARP Bulletin, a monthly newsmagazine published by the nation's largest membership organization for seniors. At the same time that homeless numbers are growing, writes Fleck, cities all over the country are cracking down on homeless people by outlawing panhandling, sitting on the sidewalk, or sleeping in public places or vehicles. Recognizing that a growing number of newly homeless people have both cars and jobs, Santa Barbara, California, is handling the situation differ-

ently by allowing homeless individuals to sleep in their vehicles in special parking lots—a much welcomed and creative approach.

As you read, consider the following questions:

1. What does Nan Roman, president of the National Alliance to End Homelessness, say is different about the recent wave of homelessness?

2. What does the "blanket ban" in Santa Cruz, California, prohibit?

3. In what designated areas are people allowed to sleep in their vehicles in Santa Barbara, California?

Behind a security gate in the desolate parking lot of a historic church in Santa Barbara, Calif., the grandmother settles in for the night in her Jeep Grand Cherokee. She reads a book, says her prayers and tucks a coat under her head before drifting off to sleep in the back seat.

No one knows she is homeless—not her coworkers at the coffee shop where she earns $8 an hour nor her colleagues at the real estate firm where she spends time each week trying to rebuild a business.

"I figured I'd always have money," says the woman, 55, who preferred to remain anonymous and recently owned two homes worth nearly $2 million. "I never dreamed this would happen."

Unable to sell her homes or shoulder the $10,000-a-month mortgage payments, she declared bankruptcy in 2005. A year later, she lost both properties, becoming an early statistic in America's foreclosure crisis.

Today she epitomizes the changing face of homelessness as a small but growing number of lower- and middle-income Americans—people who never expected to become homeless—are driven out of their homes and onto the street by the nation's economic turmoil and the record foreclosure rate.

Many of the homeless are over 50. Nan Roman, president of the National Alliance to End Homelessness in Washington [DC], says, "More people are becoming homeless when they're older, which is new. The programs that inoculated older people against homelessness are not keeping up."

A National Problem

An estimated 1.6 million people were homeless in America between October 2007 and October 2008. And they are turning up in some unlikely locales. In Kansas's suburban Johnson County, where residents have the highest median income in the state, a shelter run by the Salvation Army is operating at full capacity and has a waiting list for the first time, says spokeswoman Amanda Waters. In parts of central and south Florida, including Tampa, low- and middle-income workers are increasingly occupying shelters. The same is true in Cleveland, where emergency shelters are housing more people from higher-income exurbs like Brecksville and North Royalton.

Ironically, the thousands of homes and commercial properties lost to foreclosure and abandoned in Cleveland are serving a new purpose—providing shelter for many of the homeless who are trying to stay off the streets, says Brian Davis, executive director of the Northeast Ohio Coalition for the Homeless.

In Los Angeles, hundreds of people are living in their cars because shelters can accommodate only about a third of the city's estimated 73,000 homeless population, the largest in the nation, says Ruth Schwartz of Shelter Partnership, a local advocacy group. "There are many places you can park a vehicle for long periods of time without being noticed," she says.

Some 4,000 people age 62 or older in the region are homeless, says Schwartz. Even though nearly two-thirds have a mean monthly income of $773, mainly from Social Security, many can't make ends meet, since local housing is so expensive.

Dozens of cities have responded to the crisis by making it increasingly difficult, if not illegal, to live on the streets. No-camping and no-sleeping ordinances are pervasive in many municipalities, including Atlantic City, N.J.; Albuquerque, N.M.; Olympia, Wash.; Fresno and Ontario, Calif.; and Miami and Sarasota, Fla. Panhandling has been outlawed or restricted in Lawrence, Kan.; Atlanta; Pittsburgh, Pa.; Akron, Ohio; and Lexington, Ky.

Santa Cruz, Calif., once known for its anything-goes life-style, has implemented some of the nation's harshest laws, says attorney Kate Wells. A "blanket ban," punishable by fines, makes it unlawful for people living outside to cover themselves with a blanket from 11 p.m. to 8 a.m. Sleeping in cars is illegal during those hours. So is lingering in covered parking lots, where many people seek shelter during bad weather.

"Almost every city in the United States has tried to create new ways to make it illegal to be homeless," says Davis of the Northeast Ohio Coalition for the Homeless. "Mayors and legislators think you can legislate this out of existence."

The Santa Barbara Solution

In Santa Barbara, Calif., an ultra-affluent oceanfront city surrounded by mountains, a novel approach is being used to accommodate recently homeless people who are among the more fortunate—they work and can afford cars, gas and insurance and often retain gym memberships for a place to shower.

Every evening, a dozen private and municipal parking lots throughout the city are transformed into relatively safe outdoor lodging for 55 of the estimated 300 homeless people who sleep in their vehicles. Two social workers check the lots each night as part of a safe parking project, run by the local New Beginnings Counseling Center with funding from the city.

The Number of Elderly Homeless Is Expected to Rise

There is some troubling evidence that homelessness is beginning to increase among elderly adults. In addition, there are demographic factors—such as the anticipated growth of the elderly population as baby boomers turn 65 years of age and recent reports of increases in the number of homeless adults ages 50 to 64—that suggest a dramatic increase in the elderly homeless population between 2010 and 2020. While the country's changing demographics may make this finding unsurprising, it has serious implications for providers of homeless services and should be deeply troubling to the policy makers that aim to prevent poverty and homelessness among the elderly through local and federal social welfare programs.

M. William Sermons and Meghan Henry,
"Demographics of Homelessness Series:
The Rising Elderly Population,"
Research Matters, *Homelessness Research Institute/*
National Alliance to End Homelessness, April 2010.

For three months, Barbara Harvey, 66, slept in the lot reserved for women only. Propped up by pillows and blankets, Harvey and her two hefty golden retrievers squeezed into the back of her Honda SUV [sport-utility vehicle]. In August [2008], a friend found her a place in San Luis Obispo, 100 miles away.

A mother of three, Harvey became homeless after she lost her job as a notary and couldn't afford her $2,150-a-month rent, even with Social Security and a part-time job. But she didn't want to leave. She was familiar with the city and its resources—so she wound up in the parking lot. "Just having a place to park added stability," says Harvey. "The dogs were familiar with the area and they didn't go running off. I felt safe."

Vehicularly Housed

Among her "neighbors" were a 54-year-old woman who shared her compact car with three cats, and a 79-year-old Texan who spoke fondly of her boarding school days.

Gary Linker, executive director of New Beginnings, which modeled the parking program after one in Eugene, Ore., says the high cost of housing in places like Santa Barbara has pushed people into unexpected living situations.

"Communities are recognizing the viability of people living in their vehicles," he says. "Each may not like it, but when you look at the severe limitations of affordable housing, you've got to accept this as an option for people."

Harvey, like the grandmother in her Jeep, didn't immediately end up sleeping in her car. Each stayed with relatives, friends and in motels before they ran out of choices.

Nancy Kapp, 50, one of the social workers who checked in on Harvey, was homeless herself years ago when she was raising her daughter.

"Santa Barbara is one of the richest places in the country, and it's amazing what's happening here," says Kapp, shaking her head.

"Poverty has been going on for so long and people ignored it, but now it's hitting the middle class, and people are paying attention. We should've been trying to find solutions years ago."

> *"The number of sheltered homeless liv-*
> *ing in rural and suburban areas across*
> *the country rose from 367,551 in 2007*
> *to 509,459 in 2008, when the national*
> *economy took its dive."*

Rural Homelessness
Is a Serious Problem

Myers Reece

In the following viewpoint, award-winning journalist Myers Re-
ece highlights the growing plight of homelessness in rural areas.
Reece notes that his home state of Montana is one of the hardest
hit by the effects of the spiraling national economy. Low wages,
high rents, and an epidemic of property foreclosures and unem-
ployment all contribute to an alarming increase in rural home-
lessness, says Reece. Families, in particular, may be underrepre-
sented among the count of rural homeless, Reece maintains,
because they try to hide their situation to avoid social stigma
and shame. Families who live near the poverty line are often just
one car repair or medical bill away from not being able to pay
the rent, Reece notes, and local assistance programs are geared to

help such families get through tough times. Reece writes for the Flathead Beacon, *a weekly print newspaper and daily online news outlet in western Montana.*

As you read, consider the following questions:

1. According to the author, what are some of the issues that young single mothers with children face?

2. What docs Ellen Bassuk, president of the National Center on Family Homelessness in Massachusetts, say is the biggest driver of homelessness?

3. Does Family Promise director Gloria Edwards think homelessness is situational or chronic for most families?

The nation's rural homeless rate is soaring. In Montana, it has really grown wings. But it's not bums begging for your change on the corner. It's the kid sitting next to your child in third grade. It's your coworker. Montana's homeless are disproportionately working families. And they're crowding shelters from Billings to Kalispell.

Nationwide, families make up about 30 percent of the homeless population. In parts of Montana, the rate is double, though exact statistics are impossible for a demographic that often prefers to hide. Shelters and housing programs geared specifically toward homeless families are sprouting up all over the state, but officials say it's still far from enough. Low wages and high rent in Montana are the overriding culprits; skyrocketing foreclosure and unemployment rates aren't helping either.

According to a report by the U.S. Department of Housing and Urban Development [HUD], the number of sheltered homeless living in rural and suburban areas across the country rose from 367,551 in 2007 to 509,459 in 2008, when the national economy took its dive. That's a 39 percent jump—for rural and suburban families it was 56 percent. Larry Gallagher, with HUD's Helena field office, said Montana's rates are in step with those trends.

Across the board, Montana's homeless population is higher than most would ever guess, Gallagher said. According to the HUD report, the state's homeless rate grew in 2008 by 23.2 percent, the third-highest increase in the nation behind Mississippi (42.4) and Wyoming (39.9). Families account for a significant percentage of that total. Despite the high numbers, it's believed that homeless families, in their eagerness to avoid shame, are severely undercounted.

"We're seeing an alarming increase in homelessness in Montana," Gallagher said.

Homeless Families

By and large, homeless families—both statewide and nationally—are made up of young single mothers with kids. Some of these moms have substance abuse problems or mental illnesses, but many just can't pay the bills. They generally have low levels of education and limited job skills, but most are working, sometimes multiple jobs. Many of those who were barely hanging on before have now crumbled under the flailing economy.

At Kalispell's Samaritan House, the largest homeless shelter in Flathead County, families make up 60 percent of occupancy. The Samaritan House provides emergency shelter, transitional housing and permanent housing for up to 118 people. It's almost always full.

Eugene and Christine Welch, ages 23 and 21, say they wouldn't be able to raise their child without the Samaritan House's services. The day that their daughter Naomi was born, they left the hospital and drove directly to the Samaritan House. That was six months ago. They have been there ever since, living in one of the facility's apartments at a rate of $325 per month.

Prior to the apartment, they spent a few months in the free shelter. Eugene works at Office Max and Christine will soon work at Borders. They say, with their job skills, they can't find employment that pays enough to provide for both rent and their little girl. Eugene works between 29 and 32 hours per week at $8 an hour. After taxes, he brings in about $400 each paycheck—that doesn't go too far in the Flathead's rental market, especially with a baby to feed.

The Welches, who were high school sweethearts and graduated from Flathead High School, receive Medicaid assistance for Naomi, as well as money to help buy her baby formula. They peruse job listings daily.

"I guess that's just Montana," Eugene said. "It's hard; it's a tough place to live."

He added: "Without the Samaritan House, (Naomi) would probably be in child service custody."

In Missoula at the Joseph Residence, which offers housing for up to two years for homeless families, there is always a waiting list of at least 30 families, said Eran Fowler, director of supportive housing for Poverello [Center] Inc. Fowler emphasizes that "these are families that meet HUD requirements; they are living on the street or in their car. They are actually homeless."

The Chronically Homeless

Whereas emergency shelters often treat temporarily homeless families—people who are down on their luck and need a place to recuperate—the Joseph Residence takes in the chronically homeless. The average family at the Joseph Residence is headed by a single mother, though Fowler said she occasionally gets an "intact" family with both the father and mother.

In these cases, one parent is generally working while the other is attending some form of school. Enrolling and keeping the kids in school is a foremost priority of workers like Fowler. But the children are often far behind in class and have emotional problems.

"There's at least one or two children in your child's classroom that are homeless and you won't even know it," Fowler said.

Ellen Bassuk, president of the National Center on Family Homelessness in Massachusetts, said in the 1980s families accounted for about 1 percent of the homeless population. Over the next two decades, that figure swelled to more than 30 percent. The large increase is attributed to economic factors and shifts in the American family—there are far more single-mother families.

"The biggest driver of homelessness is poverty—female heads of family are poor," Bassuk said.

Further exacerbating matters in Montana are the state's high foreclosure rates, which are particularly prevalent in the Flathead. . . . People who have lost their homes or jobs, or both, are overwhelming aid services across the state.

Lori Botkin of the Flathead Food Bank said her agency is consistently flooded with families, many from the middle class, which represents a dramatic shift from past years. In 2008, the Flathead Food Bank distributed 18 percent more food than the previous year.

"We're not seeing the live-under-the-bridge homeless," Botkin said. "It's more middle-income families. They come in, they're well dressed; they drive nice cars."

In a recession, fragile budgets strain and then shatter. Rural families living below or near the poverty line are never too far from homelessness. Sherrie Downing, coordinator for the Montana Council on Homelessness, describes it this way: "When you're living at minimum wage you can be one car breakdown away from not being able to pay rent."

Local Solutions for Local Problems

Downing said homelessness is dangerous and can become expensive when people from the streets end up in the emergency room or short-term hospital care. The streets aren't kind to medical conditions and injuries.

"The reality is people die without having homes," Downing said. "Essentially, homelessness is a local problem that's going to require local solutions."

Montana has stepped up its programs and homeless awareness in recent years. In 2004, Gov. Judy Martz gave an executive order to establish the Montana Council on Homelessness, for which Downing works. After each legislative session since, Gov. Brian Schweitzer has re-authorized it. . . .

Also, organizations across the state are holding more events geared toward homeless awareness, as well as offering services. Over the weekend in Helena [in September 2009], Downing and Gallagher helped orchestrate one such event where homeless people were invited to shower, eat, receive dental and medical care, and learn more about available programs. These types of gatherings are increasingly common and widely attended.

There are also programs such as Family Promise, for homeless families, emerging in the state. Family Promise has a branch in Bozeman, with more planned in Helena and Missoula. As of now, there is no family-focused organization in the Flathead, leaving the Samaritan House and A Ray of Hope to shoulder the load.

It's not always easy for organizations to find homeless families, as they tend to be more ashamed than individuals and try to remain hidden, said Gloria Edwards, executive director of Bozeman's Family Promise: "They're not very visible—they're not the ones standing on street corners. But it's important to find them early before their problems grow worse. For most families, homelessness isn't a lifestyle—it's more situational than chronic," Edwards said.

"A lot of times families just need a hand up," Edwards said. "And then they can be independent again."

> *"Youth emancipating from foster care are more likely than young people in the general population to have educational deficits and experience mental health problems, economic instability, criminal victimization, and early child bearing."*

Homelessness Is a Serious Problem Among Foster Youth

Elizabeth Calvin

Children who grow up in foster care or group homes are cut off from support services when they turn eighteen and "age out" of the social services system. In the following viewpoint, youth advocate Elizabeth Calvin explains that such "emancipated" young people often end up homeless, because they are typically forced from their housing situations with no jobs, limited education, poor independent living skills, little emotional support, and few ties to the community. Calvin interviews more than sixty emancipated foster youth who became homeless in California. She uses their stories to inform her assessment of how the foster care system fails to help emancipating youths successfully transition to independent living, and she offers several recommendations for how to improve outcomes. Calvin is a senior advocate for the Children's Rights division of Human Rights Watch, an independent nonprofit organization dedicated to defending and protecting human rights around the world.

As you read, consider the following questions:

1. What percentage of emancipated foster youth do researchers estimate end up homeless?

2. What is unique about the size of California's foster youth population?

3. Why does the author say foster youth don't know how to live on their own once they are emancipated?

> On the day of my so-called emancipation, I didn't have a high school diploma, a place to live, a job, nothing. . . . The day I emancipated—it was a happy day for me. But I didn't know what was in store. Now that I'm on the streets, I honestly feel I would have been better off in an abusive home with a father who beat me; at least he would have taught me how to get a job and pay the bills.
>
> —*Roberta E., Los Angeles*

When children in foster care turn 18, they are, for the most part, on their own. "Emancipated," they are legally adults and free from the foster care system. Most entered foster care because abuse or neglect at home triggered the duty of the state to step in and protect them. The state becomes parent; in that role, it must provide special measures of protection. The state must ensure that children in foster care have adequate food, clothing, shelter, health care, and education. But no less important is the responsibility to provide the guidance and support necessary for children to grow into independent adults. When the state fails in its responsibility to protect children wholly dependent on it by not providing for their developmental needs, there are grim consequences. While exact estimates vary, research suggests that somewhere around 20 percent of the approximately 20,000 youth leaving foster care nationally each year will become homeless. For youth who leave foster care with no job or income, few educational prospects, and little emotional support or community connections, emancipation can mean nowhere to turn and no place to go.

Human Rights Watch interviewed young people who were removed as children from their family homes for abuse, neglect, or abandonment and placed in the custody and care of the state of California. After leaving foster care, they became homeless. The 63 young people interviewed had clear conclusions about the causes of their homelessness. No one pointed to a single event, nor did any interviewee wholly blame the child welfare system or another person. Instead, they pieced together a mosaic of events that spanned their teen years and early adulthood. They described missed opportunities to learn skills, the lack of the ability to support themselves, a shortage of second chances when things did not go right, and the fact that no one cared what happened to them.

From Foster Care to Homelessness

For some youth leaving foster care, homelessness comes the day they emancipate from the foster care system; others move from a foster home into a bad housing situation only to find themselves without shelter shortly thereafter. They may feel lucky to crash on a friend's couch, or they find themselves sleeping in a car, at an emergency shelter, or in the park. Some are without a steady roof over their heads for days that turn into weeks or even years. Those leaving foster care with special needs often face a particularly rough road: mental health problems or cognitive limitations can bar entry to a transitional living program. So can being a parent. Youth who are lesbian, gay, bisexual, or transgender often have even fewer community resources and support to avoid homelessness.

Too many foster children face poverty, early pregnancy, educational failure, criminal victimization, or incarceration in early adulthood. Homelessness, with its attendant dangers—including exposure to predatory crime, drugs, HIV/AIDS, and violence—is probably the worst outcome for a young person. Yet homelessness is a predictable future for many foster youth. Social workers know it. Many policy makers know it. Research confirms it. California's own Department of Social Services concluded that 65 percent of emancipating youth lack safe and affordable housing at the time of emancipation. Although conclusions as to the rate vary, homelessness is a certainty for too many youth leaving foster care.

"Built into the System"

The route from foster care to homelessness is not only well-known to the state, but is, in effect, built into the system. Social workers transport some youth directly from foster homes to emergency shelters, fully aware that these shelters will house them for limited periods before turning them out onto the streets. Others are sent to transitional living situations with no backup plan in place if things do not work out. Child welfare agencies release some youth from care when they have nowhere to live. Instead of providing extra protections for especially vulnerable youth, including mentally ill or impaired individuals and pregnant girls, state regulations often exclude them from transitional programs.

In California, 65,000 children and youth are in the foster care system, far more than any other single state. Each year, more than 4,000 emancipate. Between 2003 and 2008, over 26,500 youth emancipated from California's foster care system. If an estimated 20 percent ended up homeless, 5,300 young people went from state care to homelessness in that period of time.

California is failing in an essential duty to children in its care: to prepare them for adulthood and to survive independently. There is no magic switch that at age 18 delivers the skills, knowledge, and support necessary for survival and success. Just as the state has a duty to provide appropriate shelter, food, and health care to children in its care, it has a duty to address the crucial developmental needs of childhood and adolescence. The consequences are severe for young people who enter adulthood without this guidance and support.

No Realistic Plan for Emancipation

California state law requires child welfare agencies to develop, in conjunction with foster youth, a plan for what they will do when leaving foster care. Most of the youth Human Rights Watch spoke with had no plan when they left the system, or if one existed, they did not know about it.

In some cases, state officials fail to develop these plans at all, and in others, they create plans that are unrealistic and unlikely to prevent a youth from becoming homeless. For example, Natalie R. had three weeks left in foster care when we interviewed her. She had not yet finished high school and tests during the previous year placed her performance at an eighth-grade level. When asked if her social worker was putting together a plan with her for emancipation, she said, "Well, we're talking about college." There was no plan for where she would live or how she would support herself. Arlena C. told us, "My social worker never sat down with me to talk about emancipation. The only plan was for me to emancipate. They didn't talk about where I was going to stay after I left foster care or anything like that." She was 20 years old at the time of her interview, and had been homeless off and on since leaving care.

No Plan for Housing or the Income to Afford It

The vast majority of the young people interviewed by Human Rights Watch had no way to pay for housing at the time of emancipation: 57 of 63 young people we interviewed, or 90 percent, had no source of income when they left foster care and were expected to be on their own. They were also ill-prepared to find and hold a job: 65 percent of those interviewed had not graduated from high school at the time of emancipation. In addition, 62 percent had no medical coverage when they left the state's care, despite a legal mandate that every former foster youth should have state medical coverage until age 21.

In the last ten years [since 2000] there has been an increase of funding and an infusion of effort to improve transitional living programs in California. However, the number of places is still far too small to assist all those who need them and the funding is under constant threat. Most post-emancipation transitional living programs offer reduced rent and can provide a supportive environment in which to learn life skills. Services can include case management, assistance with education, job training and support, and mentoring. California's Transitional Housing Program-Plus (THP-Plus) was established by state law in 2001. The number of THP-Plus placements has dramatically increased: in 2003 there were places for 50 youth, by 2007 there were 502, and in 2008, 1,234 places. Yet in 2008, 4,653 youth emancipated from care.

Basic Living Skills Lacking

Tony D. told us: "If you're going to put kids in group homes, in foster care—at least give them what they need to survive and take care of themselves." We interviewed him at a homeless shelter where he was staying. "[When I aged out of care] I was expected to know how to get a job, buy a car, all that stuff, but ... I didn't have any idea how to go about doing things. So, I ended up on the street." Raul H. summed it up, "Kids need to be taught how to cook, how to shop. Simple, everyday life skills." He was 21 years old when we spoke with him, and had been homeless but now was in an apartment.

For youth in care, several things impede what otherwise would be normal opportunities for hands-on learning experiences. Foster parenting tends to be geared to the needs of younger children. Foster parents are not trained or expected to teach adult life skills to teens. Michele Phannix, an experienced foster parent and a mentor to other foster parents, told us, "There needs to be more training on teenage issues for foster parents and how to guide them into becoming functioning adults. Foster parents are not receiving that kind of training." Dr. Marty Beyer, a psychologist specializing in adolescent development and an expert on child welfare, believes those charged with caring for foster children take on a crucial role. "[T]he role that foster parents play ought to include what most parents think should be done for their children before they go off on their own." For many of the young people interviewed, however, the state failed to ensure that foster parents provided teens in their care the kind of basic living skills that would be passed on in any typical home.

Nor do group homes teach what adolescents need to learn. Interviewees pointed out that the regimented, institutionalized setting provides even fewer opportunities to learn and practice adult skills than a foster family home. Anya F. was homeless for more than two years after leaving care. She spent a good part of her teenage years in group homes, and described her experience:

> While in a group home there were so many things I couldn't do. I couldn't even learn how to ride the bus on my own— but I had to go to a class that supposedly taught me how to do normal things. It's a double standard that doesn't make sense. It's like they're saying to us "You must be independent by age 18," but then they don't give us the room to learn to be independent. Don't over-shelter us and then tell us to be independent.

While some youth in foster care participate in county-sponsored independent living skills classes, experts question the effectiveness of teaching life skills in a classroom. In any case, many of the youth interviewed for this report attended few or none of the classes, or said that they were not useful. Roberta attended just one life skills class. She described it as a last-minute cram session: "It was one week before emancipation. They gave us pots and pans, silverware. Taught us how to write a check. . . . They gave us a certificate for taking the class and we had pizza and that was it." Others who found the classes useful tended to describe hands-on teaching techniques.

No One to Turn To

One of the statements we heard most from interviewees was that no one really cared what happened to them, before or after emancipation. They expressed despair and fear about having no one to turn to after they left foster care; this lack of social support and guidance leaves young people particularly vulnerable to homelessness. While the state is obligated to aid foster youth in establishing and maintaining connections with relatives or other important figures, that did not happen for these young people. 48 of 63 youth interviewed told us they did not have an adult they could turn to in a crisis, for example, for a ride to the doctor if they were very sick. Nine said "maybe," there might have been someone they could call, but were unsure. Just six youth of the 63 young people interviewed told us they had an adult on whom they could rely. "I feel like the people who were supposed to help me weren't there for me—and I think what's going to happen to me?" one young woman said. "Am I going to live on the streets for the rest of my life?"

Support Before and After Age 18 Is Needed

An abrupt end to childhood does not comport with what is now known about adolescent development or the norms in the US. In a healthy family, preparation for adulthood begins early in life and, in most US families, youth are not cut off from support at age 18. Instead, intact families continue to provide a wide spectrum of emotional and financial support as youth move through early adulthood. As Ashley, a former foster youth, said, "[N]obody puts their real kid out at 18. It's being realistic." In contrast, youth who age out of the foster care system must survive on their own without the support available to other young adults. While some are able to make a smooth transition to adulthood, many face serious challenges. Research shows that youth emancipating from foster care are more likely than young people in the general population to have educational deficits and experience mental health problems, economic instability, criminal victimization, and early child bearing. They need support throughout early adulthood even more than the general population of young adults.

The young people interviewed for this report were currently or recently homeless former foster children. They hailed from all over California, from communities urban and rural, north and south. While there were many causes of their homelessness, their lives bear witness to the need for dramatic change in how foster youth are treated. This report is not a comprehensive review of what California's 58 counties are doing to protect and provide for children and youth in care, nor is it a survey of programs, systems, or laws. Instead, it is a lens narrowly focused on one of the system's most striking failings: the likelihood that youth in foster care will become homeless because foster care has not prepared them for adulthood.

Key Recommendations

1. **Extend support for youth in foster care beyond age 18**. Transition to adulthood should be more gradual than it currently is for youth in foster care. Financial support, adult connection, shelter, and other safety nets should be provided in a graduated way into the early 20s for youth who need it. Youth who choose to leave state care at age 18 should have opportunities to return on the basis of need.

2. **Guarantee that youth have useful emancipation plans**.
   Legally mandated "transitional independent living
   plans," which child welfare agencies are required to develop for each youth's emancipation, should incorporate
   concrete arrangements for housing, income, connection
   to others, and medical coverage.

3. **Create real opportunities for youth to develop skills
   for independence**. Everyday life skills should be taught
   in foster care at an earlier age and not just in a classroom setting. Youth should be provided opportunities
   throughout adolescence to practice tasks and skills for
   adulthood.

4. **Help youth establish relationships that extend beyond
   emancipation**. To prepare youth in foster care for adulthood, the state should help them establish relationships
   with people who can offer guidance and support
   through early adulthood.

"*LGBT youth face the threat of victimization everywhere: at home, at school, at their jobs, and, for those who are out-of-home, at shelters and on the streets.*"

Homelessness Is a Serious Problem for LGBT Youth

Nicholas Ray

The National Gay and Lesbian Task Force (NGLTF) estimates that between 20 percent and 40 percent of homeless youth are lesbian, gay, bisexual, or transgender (LGBT)—a rate many times higher than that of the general population. In the following viewpoint, NGLTF senior policy analyst Nicholas Ray explores the unique factors that contribute to homelessness among LGBT youths. Ray turns a critical eye toward the treatment of LGBT youths within mainstream social services, and he assesses the systematic failings that let such inequities emerge. Finally, Ray offers recommendations for federal, state, and local governments and social services providers.

Nicholas Ray, *Lesbian, Gay, Bisexual and Transgender Youth: An Epidemic of Homelessness*. Washington, DC: National Gay and Lesbian Task Force, 2006, pp. 1–7. Copyright © 2006 by National Gay and Lesbian Task Force. All rights reserved. Reproduced by permission.

As you read, consider the following questions:

1. What does the author say is the last resort for many homeless LGBT youths?

2. Why is the author concerned that religious charities are exempt from federal nondiscrimination laws in hiring?

3. What does the author recommend be required of all agencies that seek government funding and licensure to serve homeless youth?

The U.S. Department of Health and Human Services estimates that the number of homeless and runaway youth ranges from 575,000 to 1.6 million per year. Our analysis of the available research suggests that between 20 percent and 40 percent of all homeless youth identify as lesbian, gay, bisexual or transgender (LGBT). Given that between 3 percent and 5 percent of the U.S. population identifies as lesbian, gay or bisexual, it is clear that LGBT youth experience homelessness at a disproportionate rate. It is this reality that prompted the National Gay and Lesbian Task Force (the Task Force), in collaboration with the National Coalition for the Homeless (NCH), to produce this publication.

Through a comprehensive review of the available academic research and professional literature, we answer some basic questions, including why so many LGBT youth are becoming and remaining homeless. We report on the harassment and violence that many of these youth experience in the shelter system and we summarize research on critical problems affecting them, including mental health issues, substance abuse and risky sexual behavior. We also analyze the federal government's response to youth homelessness, including the specific impact on LGBT homeless youth of increased federal funding for faith-based service providers.

We also partnered with five social service agencies who have written sections that detail model programs they have developed to improve service delivery to LGBT homeless youth. In order to put a face to all of this research and data, we also include profiles of LGBT homeless youth, many of which were collected through focus groups we conducted at service providers around the country. Finally, in consultation with a number of youth advocacy organizations, we conclude with a series of state-, federal- and practitioner-level policy recommendations that can help to curb this epidemic.

Why Are So Many LGBT Youth Homeless?

Family conflict is the primary cause of homelessness for all youth, LGBT or straight. Specifically, familial conflict over a youth's sexual orientation or gender identity is a significant factor that leads to homelessness or the need for out-of-home care. According to one study, 50 percent of gay teens experienced a negative reaction from their parents when they came out and 26 percent were kicked out of their homes. Another study found that more than one-third of youth who are homeless or in the care of social services experienced a violent physical assault when they came out, which can lead to youth leaving a shelter or foster home because they actually feel safer on the streets.

Whether LGBT youth are homeless on the streets or in temporary shelter, our review of the available research reveals that they face a multitude of ongoing crises that threaten their chances of becoming healthy, independent adults.

LGBT homeless youth are especially vulnerable to depression, loneliness and psychosomatic illness, withdrawn behavior, social problems and delinquency. According to the U.S. Department of Health and Human Services, the fact that LGBT youth live in "a society that discriminates against and stigmatizes homosexuals" makes them more vulnerable to mental health issues than heterosexual youth. This vulnerability is only magnified for LGBT youth who are homeless.

The combination of stressors inherent to the daily life of homeless youth leads them to abuse drugs and alcohol. For example, in Minnesota, five separate statewide studies found that between 10 and 20 percent of homeless youth self-identify as chemically dependent. These risks are exacerbated for homeless youth identifying as lesbian, gay or bisexual (LGB). Personal drug usage, family drug usage, and the likelihood of enrolling in a treatment program are all higher for LGB homeless youth than for their heterosexual peers.

Survival Sex and Victimization

All homeless youth are especially vulnerable to engaging in risky sexual behaviors because their basic needs for food and shelter are not being met. Defined as "exchanging sex for anything needed, including money, food, clothes, a place to stay or drugs," survival sex is the last resort for many LGBT homeless youth. A study of homeless youth in Canada found that those who identify as LGBT were three times more likely to participate in survival sex than their heterosexual peers, and 50 percent of homeless youth in another study considered it likely or very likely that they will someday test positive for HIV.

LGBT youth face the threat of victimization everywhere: at home, at school, at their jobs, and, for those who are out-of-home, at shelters and on the streets. According to the National Runaway Switchboard, LGBT homeless youth are seven times more likely than their heterosexual peers to be victims of a crime. While some public safety agencies try to help this vulnerable population, others adopt a "blame the victim" approach, further decreasing the odds of victimized youth feeling safe reporting their experiences.

While there is a paucity of academic research about the experiences of LGBT youth who end up in the juvenile and criminal justice systems, preliminary evidence suggests that they are disproportionately the victims of harassment and

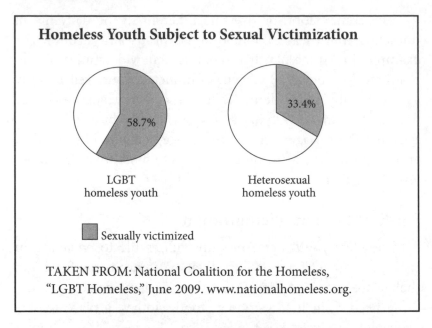

Homeless Youth Subject to Sexual Victimization

LGBT
homeless youth

58.7%

Heterosexual
homeless youth

33.4%

Sexually victimized

TAKEN FROM: National Coalition for the Homeless,
"LGBT Homeless," June 2009. www.nationalhomeless.org.

violence, including rape. For example, respondents in one small study reported that lesbians and bisexual girls are over-represented in the juvenile justice system and that they are forced to live among a population of inmates who are violently homophobic. Gay male youth in the system are also emotionally, physically and sexually assaulted by staff and inmates. One respondent in a study of the legal rights of young people in state custody reported that staff members think that "[if] a youth is gay, they want to have sex with all the other boys, so they did not protect me from unwanted sexual advances."

Transgender youth are disproportionately represented in the homeless population. More generally, some reports indicate that one in five transgender individuals need or are at risk of needing homeless shelter assistance. However, most shelters are segregated by birth sex, regardless of the individual's gender identity, and homeless transgender youth are even ostracized by some agencies that serve their LGB peers.

Obstacles to Service

Since 1974, when the federal government enacted the original Runaway Youth Act, there have been numerous pieces of legislation addressing youth homelessness. Most recently, the Runaway, Homeless, and Missing Children Protection Act (RHMCPA) was signed into law by President George W. Bush in 2003 and [was reauthorized] in 2008.

Among the most important provisions of this complex piece of legislation are programs that allocate funding for core homeless youth services, including basic drop-in centers, street outreach efforts, transitional living programs (TLPs) and the National Runaway Switchboard. While the law does not allocate funding for LGBT-specific services, some funds have been awarded to agencies who work exclusively with LGBT youth, as well as those who seek to serve LGBT homeless youth as part of a broader mission.

Unfortunately, homeless youth programs have been grossly underfunded, contributing to a shortfall of available spaces for youth who need support. In 2004 alone, due to this lack of funding, more than 2,500 youth were denied access to a TLP program for which they were otherwise qualified. Additionally, 4,200 youth were turned away from Basic Center Programs, which provide family reunification services and emergency shelter.

Lack of funding is not the only obstacle preventing LGBT homeless youth from receiving the services they need. In 2002, President George W. Bush issued an executive order permitting federal funding for faith-based organizations (FBOs) to provide social services. While more and more FBOs are receiving federal funds, overall funding levels for homeless youth services have not increased. Consequently, there is a possibility that the impact of FBOs will not be to increase services to the homeless, but rather only to change *who* provides those services.

A number of faith-based providers oppose legal and social equality for LGBT people, which raises serious questions about whether LGBT homeless youth can access services in a safe and nurturing environment. If an organization's core belief is that homosexuality is wrong, that organization (and its committed leaders and volunteers) may not respect a client's sexual orientation or gender identity and may expose LGBT youth to discriminatory treatment.

For example, an internal Salvation Army document obtained by the *Washington Post* in 2001 confirmed that ". . . the White House had made a 'firm commitment' to issue a regulation protecting religious charities from state and city efforts to prevent discrimination against gays in hiring and providing benefits." Public policy that exempts religious organizations providing social services from nondiscrimination laws in hiring sets a dangerous precedent. If an otherwise qualified employee can be fired simply because of their sexual orientation or gender identity/expression, what guarantee is there that clients, including LGBT homeless youth, will be supported and treated fairly? More research is needed on the policies of FBOs that provide services for LGBT homeless youth.

The Experiences of LGBT Youth in the Shelter System

The majority of existing shelters and other care systems are not providing safe and effective services to LGBT homeless youth. For example, in New York City, more than 60 percent of beds for homeless youth are provided by Covenant House, a facility where LGBT youth report that they have been threatened, belittled and abused by staff and other youth because of their sexual orientation or gender identity.

At one residential placement facility in Michigan, LGBT teens, or those suspected of being LGBT, were forced to wear orange jumpsuits to alert staff and other residents. At another transitional housing placement, staff removed the bedroom door of an out gay youth, supposedly to ward off any homosexual behavior. The second bed in the room was left empty and other residents were warned that if they misbehaved they would have to share the room with the "gay kid."

LGBT homeless youth at the Home for Little Wanderers in Massachusetts have reported being kicked out of other agencies when they revealed their sexual orientation or gender identity. Many also said that the risks inherent to living in a space that was not protecting them made them think that they were better off having unsafe sex and contracting HIV because they would then be eligible for specific housing funds reserved for HIV-positive homeless people in need. . . .

Policy Recommendations

This report concludes with a series of policy recommendations that can help to curb the epidemic of LGBT youth homelessness. While our focus in this publication and in these policy recommendations is to address LGBT-specific concerns, we believe that homelessness is not an issue that can be tackled piecemeal. Wholesale improvement is needed, and that is what we propose. Our recommendations are not intended to be an exhaustive list of every policy change that would make the experience of homeless youth better. Rather, we highlight some of the crucial problem areas where policy change is both needed and reasonably possible.

Federal-Level Recommendations

1. Reauthorize and increase appropriations for federal Runaway and Homeless Youth Act (RHYA) programs.

2. Permit youth who are minors, especially unaccompanied minors, to receive primary and specialty health care services without the consent of a parent or guardian.

3. Develop a national estimate of the incidence and prevalence of homelessness among American youth, gathering data that aids in the provision of appropriate services.

4. Authorize and appropriate federal funds for developmental, preventive and intervention programs targeted to LGBT youth.

5. Raise federal and state minimum wages to an appropriate level.

6. Broaden the U.S. Department of Housing and Urban Development's definition of "homeless individual" to include living arrangements common to homeless youth.

State- and Local-Level Recommendations

1. Establish funding streams to provide housing options for all homeless youth. Require that recipients of these funds are committed to the safe and appropriate treatment of LGBT homeless youth, with penalties for non-compliance including the loss of government funding. These funds would supplement federal appropriations.

2. Permit dedicated shelter space and housing for LGBT youth.

3. Repeal existing laws and policies that prevent single and partnered LGBT individuals from serving as adoptive and foster parents.

4. Discourage the criminalization of homelessness and the activities inherent to the daily lives of people experiencing homelessness.

5. Expand the availability of comprehensive health insurance and services to all low-income youth through the age of 24 via Medicaid.

Practitioner-Level Recommendations

1. Require all agencies that seek government funding and licensure to serve homeless youth to demonstrate awareness and cultural competency of LGBT issues and populations at the institutional level and to adopt nondiscrimination policies for LGBT youth.

2. Mandate individual-level LGBT awareness training and demonstrated cultural competency as a part of the professional licensing process of all health and social service professions.

3. Mandate LGBT awareness training for all state agency staff who work in child welfare or juvenile justice divisions.

Once implemented, these policy recommendations will help not only LGBT homeless youth, but all youth abandoned by their family or forced to leave home. In this report, we extensively review the academic and professional literature on the myriad challenges faced by LGBT homeless youth. The research shows that despite these challenges, many of these youth are remarkably resilient and have benefited from support from agencies like those in our model programs chapters who have worked to ensure that youth feel safe, welcome and supported. Regardless of sexual orientation or gender identity, every young person deserves a safe and nurturing environment in which to grow and learn. It is our hope that this report will bring renewed attention to an issue that has been inadequately addressed for far too long.

Periodical and Internet Sources Bibliography

The following articles have been selected to supplement the diverse views presented in this chapter.

Jessica L. Aberle	"Homelessness Not Just an 'Urban Problem,'" *Peoria Journal Star*, June 4, 2006.
Henri E. Cauvin	"Report on Homelessness Shows Increase Among Families During Recession," *Washington Post*, January 12, 2011.
Kimberly Hefling	"HUD: Rural Americans Increasingly Turn to Shelters," Associated Press, June 14, 2011.
National Coalition for the Homeless	"Who Is Homeless?," NCH Fact Sheet, July 2009. www.nationalhomeless.org.
National Student Campaign Against Hunger and Homelessness	"Communities in Crisis: A Survey of Hunger & Homelessness in America," February 2005. www.studentsagainsthunger.org.
Tony Pugh	"US Homeless Population Up Slightly, as Ranks Grow Outside Cities," *Miami Herald*, June 14, 2011.
M. William Sermons and Meghan Henry	"Demographics of Homelessness Series: The Rising Elderly Population," *Research Matters*, Homelessness Research Institute/National Alliance to End Homelessness, April 2010.
Nathan Thornburgh	"Defining 'Homelessness Down,'" *Time*, July 30, 2008. www.time.com.
US Department of Housing and Urban Development (HUD)	"2010 Annual Homeless Assessment Report to Congress," June 2011.

OPPOSING
VIEWPOINTS®
SERIES

CHAPTER 2

What Factors Contribute to Homelessness?

Chapter Preface

With the economy sputtering and unemployment at a twenty-five-year high, it's no surprise that the country's mortgage lending crisis—which has caused more than seven million home foreclosures since the economic downturn began in 2007—is an increasingly common risk factor for homelessness in the United States, especially for families.

All categories of US mortgages are at the highest default rates in history as of 2011, and as many as a quarter of all homeowners owe more on their homes than they are worth, according to RealtyTrac, a national real estate network that specializes in foreclosed properties.

A survey of homeless shelters conducted for the report *Foreclosure to Homelessness 2009: The Forgotten Victims of the Subprime Crisis*, by the National Coalition for the Homeless and other agencies, found that "a full 79 percent of respondents stated that at least *some* of their clients were homeless as a result of foreclosure, and about half estimated that more than 10 percent of their clients were homeless because of foreclosure on a home they had been occupying."

According to the 2010 Annual Homeless Assessment Report (AHAR) to Congress by the US Department of Housing and Urban Development (HUD), the economic downturn and the spike in foreclosures make certain groups more vulnerable to homelessness and are sending more families to shelters than ever before, especially in suburban and rural areas. Nearly eighty thousand family households were homeless on the night HUD conducted its point-in-time nationwide homeless count for its AHAR report. And although the annual number of people using homeless shelters in big cities decreased 17 percent since 2007, the annual number in suburban and rural areas jumped 57 percent (from 367,000 to 576,000) in the same period.

At the same time that the geography of homelessness shifted to the suburbs, the proportion of homeless family households increased, as did the percentage of white, non-Hispanic shelter users—a group not typically heavily represented in homelessness statistics.

According to the HUD report, the number of homeless family members increased 20 percent from 2007 to 2010, and families currently represent a much larger part of the total shelter population than ever before; some 35 percent of homeless people who are using emergency shelters and transitional housing are part of a family. The majority of homeless families consist of a single mother with young children, and families with children are the fastest-growing segment of the homeless population nationwide.

But the mortgage crisis is not just affecting families who have experienced foreclosure on homes they own; families who rent their homes are also being squeezed out as high mortgages force landlords to sell their rental properties or face foreclosure themselves. RealtyTrac estimates that more than 20 percent of foreclosures involve investment properties; when landlords lose those properties, their tenants lose their homes with little warning. Indeed, the *Foreclosure to Homelessness* report found that renters of foreclosed units were more heavily represented in shelters than owner-occupiers of foreclosed homes.

In 2009, President Barack Obama signed the Protecting Tenants at Foreclosure Act (Title VII of Public Law 111-22), a measure intended to ease the growing homeless crisis fueled by mortgage foreclosures. It gives renters of foreclosed properties at least ninety days to vacate, but according to the *Foreclosure to Homelessness* report, even such national protection does not resolve the problem. "Many tenants, even those who are current in their rent payments and in compliance with their leases, face an increased risk of housing loss in the wake of foreclosure proceedings," the report concluded.

Housing foreclosure is increasingly a factor that contributes to homelessness; the authors in this chapter discuss other factors that may come into play for homeless individuals and families.

"Homelessness results from a complex
set of circumstances that requires people
to choose between food, shelter, and
other basic needs."

Multiple Factors Contribute to Homelessness

National Coalition for the Homeless

As the National Coalition for the Homeless (NCH) explains in the following viewpoint, homelessness is not typically caused by any one single thing but by a variety of factors that come into play at the same time. The NCH cites a growing shortage of affordable housing and a simultaneous increase in poverty as being the main drivers of homelessness and maintains that the recent foreclosure crisis, rising unemployment rate, and decline in public assistance benefits are major contributors as well. Other factors, according to the NCH, include spiraling health care costs, mental illness, domestic violence, and addiction disorders. Since homelessness results from such a complex set of circumstances, the NCH argues, only jobs that pay a living wage, help for those who cannot work, and affordable housing and health care will bring an end to homelessness.

As you read, consider the following questions:

1. What does the NCH say are the two factors most responsible for increasing poverty?

2. What did the 2007 Conference of Mayors survey discover about homeless people and employment?

3. According to the NCH, what is the result of long waiting lists for public housing assistance?

Two trends are largely responsible for the rise in homelessness over the past 20–25 years [up until mid-2009]: a growing shortage of affordable rental housing and a simultaneous increase in poverty. Below is an overview of current poverty and housing statistics, as well as additional factors contributing to homelessness. A list of resources for further study is also provided.

Recently, foreclosures have increased the number of people who experience homelessness. The National Coalition for the Homeless released an entire report discussing the relationship between foreclosure and homelessness. The report found that there was a 32% jump in the number of foreclosures between April 2008 and April 2009. Since the start of the recession, six million jobs have been lost. In May 2009, the official unemployment rate was 9.4%. The National Low Income Housing Coalition estimates that 40 percent of families facing eviction due to foreclosure are renters and 7 million households living on very low incomes (31–50 percent of Area Median Income) are *at risk* of foreclosure.

Homelessness and poverty are inextricably linked. Poor people are frequently unable to pay for housing, food, child care, health care, and education. Difficult choices must be made when limited resources cover only some of these necessities. Often it is housing, which absorbs a high proportion of income that must be dropped. If you are poor, you are essentially an illness, an accident, or a paycheck away from living on the streets.

In 2007, 12.5% of the U.S. population, or 37,300,000 people, lived in poverty. The official poverty rate in 2007 was not statistically different than 2006. Children are overrepresented, composing 35.7% of people in poverty while only being 24.8% of the total population.

Two factors help account for increasing poverty: eroding employment opportunities for large segments of the workforce and the declining value and availability of public assistance.

Eroding Work Opportunities

Reasons why homelessness persists include stagnant or falling incomes and less secure jobs which offer fewer benefits.

Low-wage workers particularly have been left behind as the disparity between rich and poor has mushroomed. To compound the problem, the real value of the minimum wage in 2004 was 26% less than in 1979. Factors contributing to wage declines include a steep drop in the number and bargaining power of unionized workers; erosion in the value of the minimum wage; a decline in manufacturing jobs and the corresponding expansion of lower-paying service-sector employment; globalization; and increased nonstandard work, such as temporary and part-time employment. To combat this, Congress has planned a gradual minimum wage increase, resulting in the minimum wage raised to $9.50 by 2011.

Declining wages, in turn, have put housing out of reach for many workers: In every state, more than the minimum wage is required to afford a one- or two-bedroom apartment at Fair Market Rent. A recent U.S. Conference of Mayors report stated that in every state more than the minimum wage is required [for an individual] to afford a one or two-bedroom apartment at 30% of his or her income, which is the federal definition of affordable housing. Unfortunately, for 12 million

Americans, more than 50% of their salaries go toward renting or housing costs, resulting in sacrifices in other essential areas like health care and savings.

The connection between impoverished workers and homelessness can be seen in homeless shelters, many of which house significant numbers of full-time wage earners. In 2007, a survey performed by the U.S. Conference of Mayors found that 17.4% of homeless adults in families were employed while 13% of homeless single adults or unaccompanied youth were employed. In the 2008 report, eleven out of nineteen cities reported an increase in employed homeless people.

With unemployment rates remaining high, jobs are hard to find in the current economy. Even if people can find work, this does not automatically provide an escape from poverty.

Decline in Public Assistance

The declining value and availability of public assistance is another source of increasing poverty and homelessness. Until its repeal in August 1996, the largest cash assistance program for poor families with children was the Aid to Families with Dependent Children (AFDC) program. The Personal Responsibility and Work Opportunity Reconciliation Act of 1996 (the federal welfare reform law) repealed the AFDC program and replaced it with a block grant program called Temporary Assistance to Needy Families (TANF). In 2005, TANF helped a third of the children that AFDC helped reach above the 50% poverty line. Unfortunately, TANF has not been able to keep up with inflation. In 2006–2008, TANF caseload has continued to decline while food stamp caseloads have increased.

Moreover, extreme poverty is growing more common for children, especially those in female-headed and working families. This increase can be traced directly to the declining number of children lifted above one-half of the poverty line by government cash assistance for the poor.

As a result of loss of benefits, low wages, and unstable employment, many families leaving welfare struggle to get medical care, food, and housing.

People with disabilities, too, must struggle to obtain and maintain stable housing. In 2006, on a national average, monthly rent for a one-bedroom apartment rose to $715 per month which is 113.1% of [the monthly income of a person] . . . on Supplemental Security Income (SSI). For the first time, the national average rent for a studio apartment rose above the income of a person who relies only on SSI income. Recently, only nine percent of noninstitutionalized people receiving SSI receive housing assistance.

Most states have not replaced the old welfare system with an alternative that enables families and individuals to obtain above-poverty employment and to sustain themselves when work is not available or possible.

Shortage of Affordable Housing

A lack of affordable housing and the limited scale of housing assistance programs have contributed to the current housing crisis and to homelessness.

According to HUD [U.S. Department of Housing and Urban Development], in recent years the shortages of affordable housing are most severe for units affordable to renters with extremely low incomes. Federal support for low-income housing has fallen 49% from 1980 to 2003. About 200,000 rental housing units are destroyed annually. Renting is one of the most viable options for low-income people.

Since 2000, the incomes of low-income households have declined as rents continue to rise. In 2009, a worker would need to earn $14.97 [per hour] to afford a one-bedroom apartment and $17.84 [per hour] to afford a two-bedroom apartment. There has been an increase of 41% from 2000 to 2009 in fair market rent for a two-bedroom unit, according to HUD.

Federal Policies Contribute to Homelessness

Homelessness stems from systemic causes that play out via the individual biographies of people experiencing homelessness. At the epicenter of these systemic causes is over three decades of federal divestment in our afford-able housing infrastructure and programs. . . . Instead of addressing the shortage of adequate housing, federal poli-cies have only further driven the commoditization of housing as speculative asset, and in doing so led the en-tire global economy to the brink of collapse in 2008.

We can trace contemporary mass homelessness to the [Ronald] Reagan administration's destruction of the so-cial safety net and affordable housing funding. These cuts happened at the same time that the cumulative effects of deindustrialization, global outsourcing of jobs, decreasing real wages, urban renewal and gentrification were driving down income and driving up housing costs. . . . During the 1980s, . . . under Reagan's neoliberal policies, home-lessness reemerged throughout the United States.

Homeless policy has focused on a series of under-funded, patchwork efforts that tend to pit sub-populations of people experiencing homelessness, service providers and advocates against each other in battles for meager funds. Rather than addressing homelessness by providing housing options at all income levels, homeless policy in the United States has devolved into byzantine formulas used to count the number of homeless people and determine whether or not someone "qualifies" for homeless housing and services.

Western Regional Advocacy Project,
Without Housing—Decades of Federal Housing
Cutbacks, Massive Homelessness and Policy Failures.
San Francisco: Western Regional Advocacy Project, 2010.

The lack of affordable housing has led to high rent burdens (rents which absorb a high proportion of income), overcrowding, and substandard housing. These phenomena, in turn, have not only forced many people to become homeless; they have put a large and growing number of people at risk of becoming homeless.

Housing assistance can make the difference between stable housing, precarious housing, or no housing at all. However, the demand for assisted housing clearly exceeds the supply: only about one-third of poor renter households receive a housing subsidy from federal, state, or local governments. The limited level of housing assistance means that most poor families and individuals seeking housing assistance are placed on long waiting lists. Today the average wait for Section 8 vouchers is 35 months.

Excessive waiting lists for public housing mean that people must remain in shelters or inadequate housing arrangements longer. In a survey of 24 cities, people remain homeless an average of seven months, and 87% of cities reported that the length of time people are homeless has increased in recent years. Longer stays in homeless shelters result in less shelter space available for other homeless people, who must find shelter elsewhere or live on the streets. In 2007, it was found that the average stay in homeless shelters for households with children was 5.7 months, while this number is only slightly smaller for singles and unaccompanied children at 4.7 months.

In 2003, the federal government spent almost twice as much in housing-related tax expenditures and direct housing assistance for households in the top income quintile than on housing subsidies for the lowest-income households. Thus, federal housing policy has not responded to the needs of low-income households, while disproportionately benefiting the wealthiest Americans.

Other Factors Contribute to Homelessness

Particularly within the context of poverty and the lack of affordable housing, certain additional factors may push people into homelessness. Other major factors, which can contribute to homelessness, include the following:

Lack of Affordable Health Care: For families and individuals struggling to pay the rent, a serious illness or disability can start a downward spiral into homelessness, beginning with a lost job, depletion of savings to pay for care, and eventual eviction. One in three Americans, or 86.7 million people, is uninsured. Of those uninsured, 30.7% are under eighteen. In 2007–2008, four out of five people that were uninsured were working families. Work-based health insurance has become rarer in recent years, especially for workers in the agricultural or service sectors.

Domestic Violence: Battered women who live in poverty are often forced to choose between abusive relationships and homelessness. In addition, 50% of the cities surveyed by the U.S. Conference of Mayors identified domestic violence as a primary cause of homelessness. Approximately 63% of homeless women have experienced domestic violence in their adult lives.

Mental Illness: Approximately 16% of the single adult homeless population suffers from some form of severe and persistent mental illness. Despite the disproportionate number of severely mentally ill people among the homeless population, increases in homelessness are not attributable to the release of severely mentally ill people from institutions. Most patients were released from mental hospitals in the 1950s and 1960s, yet vast increases in homelessness did not occur until the 1980s, when incomes and housing options for those living on the margins began to diminish rapidly. According to the 2003 U.S. Department of Health and Human Services report, most homeless persons with mental illness do not need to be institutionalized, but can live in the community with the appropriate supportive housing options. However, many mentally ill homeless people are unable to obtain access to supportive housing and/or other treatment services. The mental health support services most needed include case management, housing, and treatment.

Addiction Disorders: The relationship between addiction and homelessness is complex and controversial. While rates of alcohol and drug abuse are disproportionately high among the homeless population, the increase in homelessness over the past two decades cannot be explained by addiction alone. Many people who are addicted to alcohol and drugs never become homeless, but people who are poor and addicted are clearly at increased risk of homelessness. Addiction does increase the risk of displacement for the precariously housed; in the absence of appropriate treatment, it may doom one's chances of getting housing once on the streets. Homeless people often face insurmountable barriers to obtaining health care, including addictive disorder treatment services and recovery supports.

Homelessness results from a complex set of circumstances that requires people to choose between food, shelter, and other basic needs. Only a concerted effort to ensure jobs that pay a living wage, adequate support for those who cannot work, affordable housing, and access to health care will bring an end to homelessness.

"There is a clear relationship between chronic homelessness and substance abuse in the United States. Addiction precipitates and sustains homelessness."

Substance Abuse Contributes to Homelessness

Regional Task Force on the Homeless

Substance abuse contributes to homelessness, and homelessness itself contributes to substance abuse, according to the following viewpoint by the Regional Task Force on the Homeless (RTFH), a nonprofit that provides research, analysis, and policy recommendations to government and social service agencies in the San Diego, California, area. The RTFH notes that homeless substance abusers often do not qualify for housing or cash benefits because of their addictions, making them more likely to live on the streets. The needs of homeless substance abusers are complex, and the RTFH maintains that assistance for this group should include services such as comprehensive health care, substance abuse treatment, transitional housing, residential programs, and comprehensive aftercare.

Regional Task Force on the Homeless, "Substance Abuse and Homelessness," *RTFH Factsheet*, July 2010. www.rtfhsd.org. Copyright © 2010 by Regional Task Force on the Homeless. All rights reserved. Reproduced by permission.

As you read, consider the following questions:

1. What does the author say is more likely to happen to a homeless person who started abusing substances only after becoming homeless?

2. What does the author assert about substance abuse among women as opposed to that among men?

3. How much money does the author claim San Diego saves taxpayers with its Serial Inebriate Program?

The relationship between homelessness and alcohol and drug addiction remains controversial. As the homeless population disproportionately represents a great number of homeless persons with addictive disorders, such disorders cannot, by themselves, explain the increase in homelessness since the 1980s. Most drug and alcohol addicts don't become homeless. However, people who must juggle very low income along with their addictive disorders are clearly at increased risk.

For many homeless persons, alcohol or other drug use provides a means to get through the day. Drug or alcohol abuse is both a cause and result of homelessness for some. The abuse of such substances may sometimes begin after an individual has become homeless, due to the fact that the street life subculture seems to have consumption of alcohol and other drugs as a norm. These individuals are twice as likely as other homeless people to be arrested or jailed, mostly for misdemeanors. They are often candidates for diversion programs that enable them to go from jail to more appropriate treatment, and housing.

The social support and family networks of these individuals usually have unraveled. Those who are members of families often have lost regular contact with their relatives or are no longer equipped to be primary caregivers.

There is no generally accepted "magic number" with respect to the prevalence of addiction disorders among homeless adults.

Special Issues Facing Those with Substance Problems

Between 2,829 and 3,112 of the homeless (not counting children in families) in the San Diego region have substance abuse issues as a primary characteristic. This represents up to 49 percent of the urban population. This number can go as high as 54% when taking into account the secondary characteristics of the remainder of the homeless population. For example, a homeless person with HIV/AIDS issues would have HIV/AIDS as their primary characteristic but may have additional secondary characteristics like substance abuse, etc. This is true with all the homeless subpopulations.

In general, substance problems are less prevalent among homeless women than among homeless men. The majority of homeless men who abuse drugs are in their late teens and twenties.

There is a clear relationship between chronic homelessness and substance abuse in the United States. Addiction precipitates and sustains homelessness. It also inhibits one's ability to work and destroys families and other social relationships. Consequently, once an abuser loses his or her source of income and housing, friends or family may be unwilling to offer assistance. In an increasingly competitive affordable housing market, drug and alcohol abusers are the last to qualify for housing benefits and thus, end up on the streets more than the rest of the low-income population. Additionally, new welfare and Social Security disability income regulations concerning alcohol and drug abusers severely limit, and in most cases, eliminate this group's eligibility for such assistance.

The San Diego Serial Inebriate Program is a collaboration between the city and county of San Diego, the San Diego Police Department and local service providers. This program addresses the needs of chronic alcoholics, many of which are chronically homeless. This program costing only a few hundred thousand dollars saves taxpayers millions in emergency room, police dept. and jail costs. . . .

Top Unmet Needs

The needs of homeless substance abusers are multiple and complex. They include access to comprehensive health care, substance abuse treatment, transitional housing, residential programs that provide on-site services to parents with substance abuse problems and their children, and innovative aftercare environments to provide a continuum of care in housing. Also needed are mental health, vocational, educational, legal, veterans and welfare services. Such support services are necessary to ensure that an individual's full range of needs is met and to help an individual maintain sobriety. The need for transportation, clothing, food and shelter is similar to that of other homeless persons. Outreach and intake services are also important in order to make services available to homeless people with alcohol problems who need them but resist accepting services.

> "Some studies have suggested that up to
> 75 per cent of the homeless population
> has a mental illness. More conservative
> research has argued [it is] between 15
> per cent and 42 per cent."

Mental Illness Contributes to Homelessness

Timothy Wild

According to the following viewpoint by public policy strategist Timothy Wild, two major factors have contributed to the large percentage of homeless people who are mentally ill. The first, writes Wild, is what he calls market failure—the tendency for already vulnerable people to become further marginalized by negative economic events such as rising rents or job loss. The second factor, according to Wild, is deinstitutionalization—the movement to remove mentally ill people from restrictive institutional settings in favor of them living in the community. Wild argues that the lack of proper community supports and services following deinstitutionalization led to a "revolving door" for the mentally ill at hospitals and jails. To address the problem, Wild emphasizes the importance of offering a wide range of services and increasing advocacy for the homeless mentally ill.

Timothy Wild, "Homelessness and Mental Illness—A Closer Look," *Perspectives*, Fall 2006, pp. 4–5. Copyright © 2006 by American Historical Association. All rights reserved. Reproduced by permission.

As you read, consider the following questions:

1. What does the author's research suggest are the two themes that contribute to homelessness among the mentally ill?

2. What does the author say failed to be put in place for mentally ill people when deinstitutionalization took place?

3. According to the author, on what is the "housing first approach" based?

Even within so-called advanced, materially affluent and compassionate societies, there has been a long history of social marginalization occasioned by the intersection of homelessness and mental illness. And while not suggesting that mental illness per se is the major cause of homelessness, it is clear that a significant portion of our homeless citizens are dealing with profound and consistent mental health concerns. Indeed, some studies have suggested that up to 75 per cent of the homeless population has a mental illness. More conservative research has argued that between 15 per cent and 42 per cent of homeless people have some kind of mental illness as defined by the criteria of the various diagnostic and statistical manuals of the American Psychological Association. Locally, a study of absolutely and relatively homeless people in Calgary indicated that between 20 per cent and 28 per cent of participants in the study had mental health issues.

Additionally, it is important to recognize the impact of factors such as emotional distress, physical health, substance abuse, environmental considerations and situational depression on the overall mental health of homeless people. As argued by [C.I.] Cohen and [K.S.] Thompson there is considerable psychosocial stress associated with homelessness, and it is often difficult to separate issues experienced by mentally ill homeless people from those of the homeless population at large. In other words, although many people may not become homeless because of mental illness, they often fall victim to poor mental health conditions caused by the unremitting stressors of homelessness. Given this, the need to consider the interaction of mental illness, mental health and homelessness is clear.

Considering the Causes

So, why are there so many people with mental illness who are homeless? The literature seems to suggest at least two general themes: market failure and deinstitutionalization. The first theme, market failure, is related to the economic location of marginalized people in a society that determines "value" largely by one's assumed relationship to the work-income nexus. Cohen and Thompson argue that the social problem is not the result of the flawed application of deinstitutionalization, but is due more to the power of dominant social groups in terms of resource allocation, as can be seen in the retrenchment of government programs, particularly in the reduction in the stock of low-income housing. Indeed, the suggestion is made that one of the primary reasons for homelessness, for both the mentally ill and the "general" homeless, is the lack of afford-able and permanent housing. For example, in Calgary, between 2004 and 2005 there was a 2.2 per cent decline in rental housing, the waiting list for subsidized housing is between 2,000 and 2,500 people and rents are increasing. Within such a market context, Cohen and Thompson argue the division between homeless people who are mentally ill and homeless people as a broader category is largely illusory, and that many of the same factors and problems plague both the sub- and the larger population. "Thus, along with other homeless groups, the homeless mentally ill must first be seen as impoverished and disenfranchised, rather than diseased."

The second, and admittedly more widely held view, is related to the consequences of deinstitutionalization, whereby people confined to mental health institutions were afforded the opportunity to reside in the community. However, the promise of deinstitutionalization, which offered greater opportunities to participate in the broader community and avoid many of the negative factors associated with long-term confinement to an institution, together with providing savings to the public purse, foundered. There was a failure to provide the necessary community supports and services—including affordable housing—to help people with mental illness to remain authentically within the "community." It has been argued that the process of deinstitutionalization was actually a process of "transinstitutionalization" with people being faced with the "revolving door" of readmissions to hospitals and prisons and leading "marginal lives in the community."

Turning Toward Solutions

However, regardless of the "cause," and given the prevalence and incidence of mental illness and homelessness, it is important to consider what needs to occur to mitigate at least some of the problems. Not surprisingly, a number of authors have argued that the key can be found in the provision of stable and permanent housing. As noted by [researcher P.] Dattalo "mentally ill people without permanent housing have needs that cannot be met by most shelter-based organizations." Also, there is evidence to support the effectiveness of a "housing first approach" whereby people have their basic, instrumental needs met prior to receiving mental health and substance abuse treatment. Such an approach is based upon a recognition of the importance of consumer choice, voluntary participation and state-of-readiness in terms of dealing with the variety of factors that categorize mental illness and homelessness. Granted, this is somewhat at odds with programs that require a commitment to compliance prior to entry to the program. Nevertheless, [there is] evidence that the housing first approach has positive results in terms of integration and stabilization and reflects the preference of mental health consumers.

A Consortium of Care

That having been said, housing is a necessary, but by no means adequate, step. Along with the provision of a variety of housing options, services to homeless people with mental health issues should be offered along a continuum starting with emergency services, including shelter, then moving to transitional services, such as training and therapy and, finally, stabilization services, such as permanent housing and employment. [Some authors] report on the success of a community support systems framework that offered a range of services including outreach, treatment, medical and dental, crisis, housing, income, peer and family supports. [Others] comment upon the importance of assertive outreach and the building of rapport with homeless people who are mentally ill. Additionally, skills training, social supports at a variety of levels and intensities, and an active lifestyle are considered important in terms of enhanced community adjustment. A number of authors also comment upon the need to provide complementary programming that is specifically targeted in terms of working with physical abuse, substance abuse, and trauma. Finally, once again speaking of instrumental needs, it is important to recognize the need for adequate income and awareness of what income support programs are available.

Advocacy Is Key

However, implementation of the above requires significant change in both policy and public discourse. As a society it is imperative that we act to ensure that social policies and programs are put in place that both provide the necessary community-based supports and services for people with mental illness and also provide an adequate stock of low-cost housing to end the social crime of homelessness. Therefore, advocacy, at both the individual and systemic levels, must remain a central theme in resolving some of the many social issues associated with mental illness and homelessness. [Researchers P. Timms and T. Borrell suggest,] "Political embarrassment has been the major engine behind funding for specialist services for homeless people." That might well be the case, and the recent Calgary Homeless Count, which enumerated 3,436 homeless individuals in one night, may serve as a motor for change in terms of broader issues of homelessness. The time to act is now!

| "Studies from across the country confirm the connection between domestic violence and homelessness and suggest ways to end the cycle in which violence against women leads to life on the streets."

Domestic Violence Often Leads to Homelessness

American Civil Liberties Union

The Women's Rights Project of the American Civil Liberties Union (ACLU) keeps a close eye on the issue of domestic violence and how it contributes to homelessness for women and their children. In the following viewpoint, the ACLU explains how landlords with "zero tolerance for crime policies" often evict women who experience domestic violence—in effect victimizing them for a second time. Federal laws put in place to address such inequities are insufficient, the ACLU maintains, because they only protect individuals who live in public housing or whose rent is paid with public assistance. Women who are experiencing poverty or live in poor neighborhoods, notes the ACLU, are much more likely to become victims of abuse and also more likely to become homeless.

American Civil Liberties Union, "Domestic Violence and Homelessness Factsheet," ACLU Women's Rights Project, February 2008. www.alcu.org. Copyright © 2008 by American Civil Liberties Union (ACLU). All rights reserved. Reproduced by permission.

As you read, consider the following questions:

1. What does the author say a Michigan study found about women who had experienced recent or ongoing domestic violence?

2. According to the author, how much more likely are women with very low incomes to experience domestic violence than women with incomes over $75,000?

3. Why does the author say a 2005 federal law stops short of protecting many domestic violence victims?

When women flee domestic abuse, they are often forced to leave their homes, with nowhere else to turn. Landlords also sometimes turn victims of domestic violence out of their homes because of the violence against them. For years, advocates have known that domestic violence is a primary cause of homelessness for women and families. Studies from across the country confirm the connection between domestic violence and homelessness and suggest ways to end the cycle in which violence against women leads to life on the streets.

Housing instability and a lack of safe and affordable housing options heighten the risks for women experiencing domestic violence.

A lack of alternative housing often leads women to stay in or return to violent relationships. In Minnesota in 2003, for instance, 46 percent of homeless women reported that they had previously stayed in abusive relationships because they had nowhere to go. In 2003, in Fargo, North Dakota, 44 percent of homeless women reported that they stayed in an abusive relationship at some point in the past two years because they did not have other housing options.

In addition to physical violence, abusers also typically use other strategies to exercise power and control over their partners and to isolate their partners from support networks. As a result, a woman who has experienced domestic violence will often have little or no access to money and very few friends or family members to rely on if she flees a violent relationship.

The Role of Landlords

Many landlords have adopted policies, such as "zero tolerance for crime" policies, that penalize victims of domestic violence. These policies allow landlords to evict tenants when violence occurs in their homes, regardless of whether the tenant is the victim or the perpetrator of the violence. A Michigan study of women currently or formerly receiving welfare found that women who had experienced recent or ongoing domestic violence were far more likely to face eviction than other women.

Some landlords are unwilling to rent to a woman who has experienced domestic violence. For example, a 2005 investigation by a fair housing group in New York City found that 28 percent of housing providers either flatly refused to rent to a domestic violence victim or failed to follow up as promised when contacted by an investigator posing as a housing coordinator for a domestic violence survivor assistance program.

Landlords often only learn about domestic violence when victims seek help from the police or the courts. When victims know that they may face eviction if a landlord finds out about the abuse, they are less likely to seek assistance and more likely to submit to the abuse.

Domestic Violence and Poverty

Poor women, who are more vulnerable to homelessness, are also at greater risk of domestic violence. Poverty limits women's choices and makes it harder for them to escape violent relationships. . . .

While women at all income levels experience domestic violence, poor women experience domestic violence at higher rates than women with higher household incomes. Women with household incomes of less than $7,500 are 7 times as

Domestic Violence and Homelessness Facts

- In 2005, 50 percent of U.S. cities surveyed reported that domestic violence is a primary cause of homelessness. . . .

- A 2003 survey found that one-quarter of homeless mothers had been physically abused in the past year and almost all had experienced or witnessed domestic violence over their lifetimes.

- Forty-seven percent of homeless school-aged children and 29 percent of homeless children under five have witnessed domestic violence in their families. . . .

- A 1997 survey of homeless parents in ten cities around the country found that 22 percent had left their last residence because of domestic violence. . . .

- In San Diego, almost 50 percent of homeless women are domestic violence victims. . . .

- A study of family homelessness in Massachusetts found that 92 percent of homeless women had experienced severe physical and/or sexual assault at some time in their lives. One-third of homeless women were current or recent victims of domestic violence.

- A 2003 Florida study found that 46 percent of domestic violence survivors reported that they had experienced homelessness as a result of the violence. . . .

- In 2005 in Iowa, nearly a quarter of all homeless households in the state reported that they were homeless because of domestic violence.

American Civil Liberties Union,
"Domestic Violence and Homelessness Factsheet,"
ACLU Women's Rights Project, February 2008.

likely as women with household incomes over $75,000 to experience domestic violence.

Women living in rental housing experience intimate partner violence at three times the rate of women who own their homes.

Women living in poor neighborhoods are more likely to be the victims of domestic violence than women in more affluent neighborhoods. Indeed, women in financially distressed couples who live in poor neighborhoods are twice as likely to be victims of domestic violence as women in equally financially distressed relationships living in more affluent neighborhoods.

Protecting Battered Women's Homes

One way to reduce the risk of homelessness for domestic violence victims is to protect them from housing discrimination on the basis of domestic violence. For this reason, the American Bar Association (ABA) has urged lawmakers to prohibit this form of discrimination. As the report accompanying the ABA's recommendation explained, "Until we stop asking women to choose between being beaten and being able to feed and shelter their children, we cannot expect to rid our society of domestic violence."

In 2005, a federal law was adopted prohibiting many kinds of discrimination against victims of domestic violence who live in public housing or Section 8 housing. This law states, for instance, that being a victim of domestic violence is not a reason for eviction from public housing or loss of a housing voucher. This law, however, does not address discrimination in other kinds of housing against individuals who have experienced domestic violence.

Some states, most notably Washington, Rhode Island, and North Carolina, have adopted broader laws specifically prohibiting housing discrimination against domestic violence victims. Most states, however, either have no laws at all explicitly protecting domestic violence victims' housing rights or have laws that offer only narrow protection in certain circumstances. Some states, for instance, only prohibit evicting those victims of domestic violence who have obtained restraining orders against their abusers. While states are moving in the right direction, these kinds of technicalities limit many state laws' effectiveness in reducing domestic violence and subsequent homelessness.

> "The homeless rate in New Orleans has skyrocketed in the years since Katrina. According to the Brookings Institution, the city now has 12,000 homeless people, more than double the amount present before the storm."

Natural Disasters Can Lead to Homelessness

Seth Fiegerman

When Hurricane Katrina slammed into New Orleans on August 29, 2005, both the city and its residents were forever changed. In the following viewpoint, written five years after the devastating storm, journalist Seth Fiegerman explores Katrina's long-term impacts on housing and homelessness in New Orleans. As Fiegerman notes, not only did the city's population drop dramatically after the storm, but also a large percentage of those who remained were—or still are—effectively homeless. Although the federal government provided free trailers to house some displaced residents, Fiegerman writes, years of red tape and broken promises mean many people are still homeless or living in temporary housing. Additionally, Fiegerman notes that both housing prices and the number of foreclosures have increased significantly since Katrina, displacing more residents and making affordable housing even harder to find in the city than it was before the storm.

As you read, consider the following questions:

1. What kind of problems does the author attribute to living in FEMA trailers?

2. What does the author say was the effect of the Road Home program launched by Louisiana governor Kathleen Babineaux Blanco?

3. What were many public housing developments replaced by following Hurricane Katrina?

It took Charles King and his family just a couple of hours to leave their house in New Orleans on Aug. 27, 2005, but they have been struggling for five years since then to find home again.

It was two days before Hurricane Katrina struck the city, and King, 48, his wife Rosalind, 47, and their 14-year-old son managed to flee New Orleans amid bumper to bumper traffic, heading north to Baton Rouge. The family took shelter there, initially staying with relatives and starting what would become a burdensome routine of jumping from one temporary residence to the next.

Two weeks later, the family moved on to Houston, along with tens of thousands of others displaced from the Gulf Coast. During the first few weeks, they spent their days in the Astrodome scrounging for supplies and their nights cramming into a relative's apartment. They soon found an apartment of their own for two months, after which they moved again to the other side of the city to a building where the rent was covered by a voucher from the federal government.

"It was definitely a struggle. I found a couple of little odd jobs driving trucks, but not much," King says. "I just wanted to get back home."

Hurricane Katrina struck land on Aug. 29, 2005, and over the course of 15 hours, caused a massive surge of water from surrounding canals to burst through the levee system and flood the low-lying city. Investigations afterwards found that the levees were not properly designed to protect against such a strong storm, and some were not even completely built when Katrina hit. On top of that, the soil underneath the levees proved to be more unstable than expected and started to sink during the storm, which helped the incoming water push past the levees.

A few weeks later, Hurricane Rita hit, causing even more damage. At the very end of September, a small segment of the city reopened to businesses and residents, but many of the displaced had to wait months and sometimes even years to gather the resources—and the willpower—to come back.

The Population Was Cut in Half

The year after the storm hit, the population of New Orleans dropped by more than half from 455,188 to a little more than 200,000. Though the city has gradually seen many old residents return along with some newcomers, the population today is still about 100,000 fewer than it was before Katrina.

Yet some couldn't wait years to return home. King needed to earn a living for his family and believed the best place for him to do that was back in New Orleans. So by February 2006, he decided to make his way back to the city alone, leaving his family behind in Houston, where they stayed for another six months as their son finished up middle school. In that time, King found work driving dump trucks to remove slabs from demolished homes, a job he still has today, and spent his nights sleeping in a relative's trailer. In August, Rosalind and the couple's younger son finally moved back to New Orleans to join King, as did their older son, now 24, who had been working out of state.

But it was King who, nearly half a year after Katrina hit, became the first member of the family to lay eyes on the mobile home in which they'd lived for 20 years. To his horror, he found that water had settled two feet from the ceiling, destroying everything inside and rendering the home itself uninhabitable. All that was salvageable after the storm was a cooking pot and a ten-speed bicycle.

"I was devastated and couldn't believe it. This was everything I owned," King said. Although, as he manages to add with a touch of humor, "It was a real good bike."

Living in Limbo

Now, five years after their home was destroyed, the King family is among hundreds of residents who still live in emergency assistance trailers, waiting for grants to come through so they can move into a permanent residence and have their lives return to some degree of normalcy.

The King family first moved into a trailer provided by the Federal Emergency Management Agency [FEMA] back in late 2006. It was short on space so the parents shared a tiny bedroom area while their two kids slept on a makeshift sofa bed that doubled as a table during the day. After a year, FEMA allowed them to move into a more spacious three-bedroom trailer, but the government agency soon started to badger the family to move out.

"Every other week, they said we need to get out. They'd say another storm may be coming and it wouldn't be responsible for us to stay in the trailer," Rosalind recalls. "They said it was just meant to be a temporary thing."

Unfortunately, there were few homes in the city available to rent at the time and even if there had been, the family had little money. So FEMA eventually decided on a solution that would both absolve the agency of responsibility for the family and appease them. They sold Rosalind the trailer for just $5.

"There's been more pressure over the last two years where the government has threatened to take [the trailers] away," said Zack Rosenburg, co-founder of the St. Bernard Project, an organization that helps rebuild homes in New Orleans. "So what happened? Instead of facing imminent homelessness, some people decided to take control and move into apartments that they couldn't afford while others bought the FEMA trailers."

Trailers for Sale or Rent

In the weeks immediately after the storm, FEMA rolled out 120,000 trailers to help shelter many of those displaced along the Gulf Coast. These trailers were often overly cramped and in some cases may have even been a health hazard as residents complained of formaldehyde fumes coming from the walls and cabinets, causing nausea and allergic reactions.

By 2007, the number of residents relying on these temporary homes had declined by more than half, with approximately 45,000 families living in FEMA trailers. Today, FEMA reports there are 860 families in Louisiana who are still living in FEMA trailers, but Rosenburg says this estimate does not include families, like the Kings, who decided to buy their trailers. Earlier this year, FEMA auctioned off the majority of the 120,000 trailers, often for $2,000 or more.

Beyond this, there are thousands of others who may not wake up in a FEMA trailer each morning, but have yet to move into permanent housing.

"There are also about 6,000 families who own homes but can't afford to rebuild them. So they live in gutted houses or partially rebuilt homes, or else live in rentals that they can't sustain. Some simply double up with family members," Rosenburg said.

Perhaps for this reason, the homeless rate in New Orleans has skyrocketed in the years since Katrina. According to the Brookings Institution, the city now has 12,000 homeless people, more than double the amount present before the storm.

So why, after five years, are so many families still without a proper home? To answer this question, it's important to understand the sheer scope of the city's destruction.

Dealing with the Devastation

In total, nearly three-quarters of all housing units in New Orleans (134,564 to be exact) were damaged or destroyed by Hurricanes Katrina and Rita, according to FEMA's records. To deal with so much devastation, Louisiana's governor at the time, Kathleen Babineaux Blanco, developed the Road Home program, which officially launched on the one-year anniversary of Katrina and has since become the largest and most ambitious housing recovery program in this country's history.

With the help of more than $14 billion in government funding, Road Home has successfully paid out nearly 128,000 grants so far to homeowners statewide, an impressive amount by any standard. However, some have criticized this program—and the government's response as a whole—for failing to help the poorer sections of New Orleans as much as it did the wealthier areas.

"While Katrina was very much an equal opportunity disaster that hit both rich neighborhoods and poor, rich neighborhoods have largely rebounded, but poor neighborhoods still need help," said Lauren Anderson, CEO [chief executive officer] of the Neighborhood Housing Services of New Orleans, a group that offers residents financial advice and helps build and renovate homes. "The formula that was used [to allocate funds] was based not just on the extent of damage to the house, but also on pre-Katrina property values, which skewed resources in favor of wealthier homes and neighborhoods." This meant that poorer neighborhoods like the Ninth Ward, which was hit the worst by the storm, received less money than the damage warranted.

Christina Stephens, a spokesperson for Road Home, admits the program hasn't been perfect. In hindsight she says, "We probably would have designed a slightly simpler program to speed things up faster." However, she insists that Road Home and others have worked hard to assist the poorer communities. In particular, she points to a $1 billion government grant specifically intended to help improve low- to moderate-income families.

"Road Home grants are calculated a lot of times based on the pre-storm value of homes," Stephens says, echoing Anderson's point. "So we want to make sure we are helping lower income families get the funds they need."

Money to Rebuild

Residents in New Orleans are able to receive a maximum of $150,000 through the Road Home Foundation to rebuild their homes as well as an extra $130,000 through a national flood insurance program and a hazard mitigation program intended to fortify homes against future environmental threats. However, Stephens says that the average applicant ends up receiving less than half of that maximum amount.

But according to Stephens and several other nonprofits we spoke with, two of the biggest factors that have caused many families to still be homeless—besides funding—are contractor fraud and getting the proper legal documents in order.

In the first year after Katrina, the number of complaints about contractor cons in New Orleans jumped up by more than 8% as scammers quickly realized there was a big market for home repairs following the storm.

Families spent their grant money, often dipping into their savings to renovate their homes only to find out that jobs had been done incorrectly. One of the most common menaces to Louisiana homeowners has been Chinese drywall. As luck would have it, this cheap substitute to regular drywall arrived en masse in the U.S. shortly after Katrina hit. As a result, deceitful contractors and desperate homeowners often padded their houses with it. Unfortunately, this drywall wears away easily, emits a terrible odor and can lead to health problems.

Kenneth and Barbara Wiltz, two New Orleans residents in their mid-60s, experienced this issue firsthand. The couple returned to the city in 2006, bought a damaged home that was more affordable, and hired a contractor to fix it up. After the job was done, the Wiltzes found the contractor had used the wrong drywall, and had no choice but to do what many others have done: tear it all down. They reached out to Zack Rosenburg at St. Bernard Project for help.

"When we got to them, they were living in a house that only had insulation," Rosenburg says. "It was heartbreaking seeing these two folks eating dinner together at a card table with just insulation on the walls." Fortunately, Rosenburg's organization was able to make the home right again, but many others are still left with half-finished homes.

As for the other big obstacle families have faced—getting their legal papers in order—this has proved to be the major setback for the King family. While they owned the mobile home that had been destroyed in the storm, they did not own the land it sat on. Instead, the land was given to them unofficially by Charles King's uncle, who since passed away. That meant they didn't have the legal documents to show proof of ownership to organizations like Road Home.

"Due to them being family, we didn't have anything in writing. In those days and times, it was just considered family land," Rosalind says. "And Road Home had standards. If the property that the home was on was not owned by the person, well there was only so much money you could get."

This has turned out to be a relatively unique challenge to New Orleans, which historically has many residents who reside on property that had been informally passed down over the years from one family member to the next.

As Stephens, the Road Home spokesperson, explains, without the documents, "Legally, the succession had never been done." So in order to process the claim, the organization would have to painstakingly contact every member of the family with a tie to the land in order to get them to sign off on any repairs that would be made. In some cases, this drastically extended the time it took to get people into a permanent livable home.

The Cost of Moving Back Home

An odd effect of the post-Katrina recovery is that New Orleans has become less affordable. Many of the city's public housing developments were damaged in the storm and subsequently torn down and replaced by mixed-income facilities. Similarly, the median price of homes increased significantly from $137,400 in 2004 to more than $160,000 last year [2009], according to the National Association of Realtors.

According to the Brookings Institution, more than half of the poor population that once lived in the city proper has now been forced to move out to the suburbs because New Orleans has become too pricey. In fact, Brookings found that nearly 60% of all renters in the city now use up at least 35% of their income on housing costs compared to 43% who did so the year before the storm.

One of the key financial considerations for prospective homeowners in the city going forward is the issue of insurance rates. As James Donelon, Louisiana's insurance commissioner, explained to MainStreet, home insurance rates increased by 12.5% statewide the year after the storm and by an astounding 48% in New Orleans. Much of this was due to the fact that two big insurance companies, Allstate and State Farm, significantly decreased the number of policies they approved and AAA left the state all together, forcing families to pay a higher premium to the handful of companies that were willing to provide the necessary coverage.

Home insurance rates have continued to inch up in the years since, increasing by about 3%–5% statewide each year, but Donelon sees these more modest increases as a sign that rates have mostly stabilized now. And he attributes this mainly to the fact that 12 new insurance companies have started doing business in the state, and specifically along the coastal areas, since Katrina. Still, Louisiana is always near the top of the list of most expensive states for insuring homes, with an average annual premium of more than $1,000.

That doesn't even begin to take into account the cost of flood insurance, which is what most residences in the New Orleans area need most. Average premiums are about $570 a year though for more expensive homes near coastal areas, it can be much more.

Hindsight Is 20–20

"Only 40% of victims of Rita and Katrina had flood insurance in place and though there's been a slight increase since then, it's still only about 30% of properties that have it now," Donelon said, before adding, "Even though I tell the public

constantly that that's the best insurance in the state for property owners because it's subsidized by the federal government."

The King family was one of the many that did not have
any insurance on their home before the storm. "We never
thought Katrina would take everything," Rosalind reasoned,
but admitted that the next time around, they will buy the
proper insurance, no matter the extra cost.

After years of wrangling with Road Home for funds, they
successfully received a grant for enough to buy themselves a
new one-story home in June. "We said, we've just got to buy a
home before this money gets away from us, so we found a
place quickly and paid cash for it," Charles says.

The home they bought sits just five minutes from the
trailer they live in now, but when they bought it, it was completely gutted, without any walls. So for now, the family is ap-
plying for help from St. Bernard Project to fix it up. With any
luck, the family hopes they'll be able to move in to the home
in the next month or two, but until then, they will continue
to live their day-to-day lives in the shadow of what will hope-
fully become their permanent home.

For all that they've gone through, Mrs. King continues to
be optimistic about the future. Her attitude may come the
closest to summing up the spirit and mind-set of New Orleans as a whole.

"We've lost a lot," King says, "but a new beginning is better than none at all."

> *"Nationwide, suffering during the recession followed a straight . . . line from poorest to richest, with the poorest enduring catastrophic job losses, those in the middle enduring significant though less pervasive job losses and the richest enjoying scarcely a blip."*

The Economic Recession Is Increasing Homelessness

Lizzy Ratner

In the following viewpoint, journalist Lizzy Ratner examines economic disparities in New York City and uses her findings to frame a larger discussion about the nationwide recession and sputtering recovery. As goes New York, she argues, so goes the rest of the nation, and her report highlights a deepening rift between rich and poor: increasing homelessness, long lines at food pantries, and crippling unemployment for the poor, while the rich feel little or no impact. Ratner explores the recession's "unequal grip," and she takes a critical look at whether, by bailing out corporations and banks rather than the jobless, homeless, and needy, the federal government's economic stimulus money went to the wrong people.

As you read, consider the following questions:

1. What criticism does political scientist C. Nicole Mason have about the economic bailout?

2. What does the author mean by the expression "underutilized workers"?

3. What group does labor economist Andrew Sum believe should be the focus of stimulus money?

In December, as 2010 glittered to a close, life among New York City's affluent caste looked remarkably like the go-go good old days before the recession. At the opening bell of the New York Stock Exchange on December 1, Citigroup executives, apparently unfazed by their role in the financial crisis, clapped heartily as they celebrated the initial public offering of CVOL, a complex new financial product they had cooked up. At Sotheby's, collectors at the Magnificent Jewels auction snapped up more than $49 million worth of gilded baubles (including a 27.2 carat Tiffany diamond necklace that sold for more than $3.6 million), making it Sotheby's highest grossing jewelry sale ever. And at Harry Cipriani, natty-looking power-lunchers waited two deep at the bar for a table, boosting a business that only two years earlier had been troubled enough that management had considered closing off nearly half the restaurant.

"Now it's busy, as you can see," says Maggio Cipriani, the Cipriani dynasty's 21-year-old magnate in training. "We're picking up a lot."

Nearly 100 blocks north, in the heart of central Harlem, the picture is noticeably different. Things are not picking up, at least not for Pamela Brown, 51, a poised mother of three who has recently moved into the neighborhood after losing her apartment in the Bronx. Sitting at a local Starbucks, her hair pulled into an elegant twist as if she was about to head to the office, she describes how she was downsized from her administrative job at Bank of America during the great melt-down of 2008 and has struggled unsuccessfully to find work ever since. Is her age to blame, she wonders? Race? The fact that she is still a few credits shy of a college degree?

Whatever the reason, she is getting by on food stamps and welfare, her monthly income reduced to $818 for her family of three. Soap and dry cleaning are luxuries; her youngest son has left his private school. As part of the 1996 welfare "re-form" requirements, she spends her days sweeping streets for the city's mandatory Work Experience Program. "[My friends] have this false sense that I must have done something wrong for this to happen to me," says Brown. "But I did everything that I thought I was supposed to do."

Such are the stories of recession and recovery wafting up from New York's sidewalks these days.

On the one side are tales of prosperity and excess, of New York as the poster child for an economic comeback so robust that Manhattan is now the fastest growing local economy in the country. On the other side are privation and struggle.

A Story of Disparities

These disparate realities rarely elbow their way into the same conversation, but they are very much part of the same story, perhaps *the* story of recession New York. In this story, African American men lost jobs at four times the clip of their white counterparts; their unemployment rate jumped 9 points, to 17.9 percent, the largest increase of any group during the re-cession. At the same time, the median salary of managers and professionals leaped 9.5 percent, while non-managers and nonprofessionals saw their wages tumble some 4.3 percent. And according to the New York City Coalition Against Hun-ger, the city's fifty-seven billionaires (including its billionaire in chief, Mayor Michael Bloomberg) increased their collective net worth by $19 billion between 2009 and 2010, while the number of New Yorkers visiting food pantries ballooned by

200,000 during roughly the same period. Call it the trickle-down recovery that has yet to trickle down.

New York City is not an aberration; it's just one of the more dramatic examples of the recession's unequal grip. As labor economists Andrew Sum and Ishwar Khatiwada argued in a February 2010 paper, "A true labor market depression faced those in the bottom two deciles of the income distribution, a deep labor market recession prevailed among those in the middle of the distribution, and close to a full employment environment prevailed at the top. There was no labor market recession for America's affluent." No wonder 2009 set records for income inequality. In that year, the chasm between rich and poor measured even wider than it did in 1928, the last time so much wealth was concentrated in so few hands.

The Gap Between Rich and Poor

Even before the Great Recession, all was not as sunny as it seemed in New York City. For the lucky minority, the boom years of the 1990s and 2000s were glorious times. As the twin forces of financial deregulation and corporate-friendly tax policies loosened the economic floodgates, Wall Street surged, lifting all yachts if not all boats. Between 1990 and 2007, average Wall Street salaries (including bonuses) ballooned nearly 112 percent, from just over $190,000 in 1990 to more than $403,000 in 2007, according to a startling new study by the Fiscal Policy Institute. During the same period, the top 5 percent of income earners—those making more than $167,400 a year in 2007—nearly doubled their share of the city's total income, from 30 percent to 58 percent.

But for the remaining 95 percent, life was not so charmed. As unions came under assault, the minimum wage stagnated, manufacturing jobs were shipped overseas, New York's poor and working class struggled, and its middle class wasted away. As the Fiscal Policy Institute study shows, the median hourly wage shriveled 8.6 percent between 1990 and 2007. The gap between rich and poor yawned wider—while the rich claimed ever larger chunks of the pie, the poorest 50 percent claimed less than 8 percent of the city's annual income and the once robust middle claimed just above 34 percent, earning New York the honor of being the most unequal large city in America.

"If New York City were a nation, it would rank fifteenth worst among 134 countries with respect to income concentration, in between Chile and Honduras," writes James Parrott, chief economist for the Fiscal Policy Institute, in his report "Grow Together or Pull Further Apart? Income Concentration Trends in New York."

Such was the world that existed before the recession even struck, and it bore an uncanny resemblance to the Big Apple on the eve of the Great Depression, when the gap between rich and poor was epically wide. New Deal policies helped usher in an age of unprecedented (if still relative) equality after the Depression, but it seems unlikely that the same result will come from this meltdown. In fact, it seems to be exacerbating inequality.

Untangling the Reasons

The reasons for this are many and tangled. They lie in the foreclosure crisis, which fell disproportionately on minorities. They lie in the fact that the hardest-hit industries—construction, manufacturing, retail trade and administrative support services—were those that employed the poor, the working classes and struggling middle. They lie in the apparent willingness of professionals and managers to slash everyone's job but their own (Andrew Sum found no net loss in the combined number of managers and professionals employed in the country during the recession). But fundamentally, the reasons lie in policy: in a bailout that went too far and a stimulus that didn't go far enough.

"There was an over-focus on Wall Street and business, and not enough attention paid to the people that are actually integral to getting the economy going again," says C. Nicole Mason, a political scientist and executive director of New York University's Women of Color Policy Network. Sum is more blunt. "Low-income people needed the most help, and they got the least help," he said. "Nobody's bailed out the American worker."

By now, the Wall Street component of this story is well-known. Determined to prop up the imploding banking sector, the government mainlined money into Wall Street's ready veins, $193 billion through TARP [Troubled Asset Relief Program] alone. With scarcely a qualm, it gobbled up bad assets, restored the commercial paper market and saved the money market/mutual funds industry—to stunning effect. Banks did not merely survive; they earned record profits. The stock market swooped upward. And for a select sliver of New York's population, the most obvious signs of the recession seemed to melt away.

Once again, the statistics tell the story. According to the Fiscal Policy Institute, during the third quarter of 2009, denizens of Manhattan's tony Upper East and West Sides enjoyed a barely recessionary unemployment rate of 5.1 percent while residents of Brooklyn's East New York neighborhood suffered near-depression levels of unemployment (the official rate was 19.2 percent). More shocking: The unemployment rate for white men in the west Brooklyn neighborhoods stretching from Brooklyn Heights to Red Hook floated at 3 percent while black men in the same neighborhood suffered an unemployment rate of 46 percent.

"If you're sitting in financial services, you feel like it's stabilized, you feel like we're out of crisis mode," says Adam Zoia, founder and CEO [chief executive officer] of Glocap Search, a financial services head-hunting firm. Hiring is up about 30 percent from 2009, he reports, and the amount of assets under hedge fund management is back to its prerecession high of $1.7 trillion. "The compensation levels have largely recovered," he adds.

The Effect of Stimulus Spending

Unfortunately for those outside the finance sector and its satellite industries, the benefits of this comeback have largely been elusive. The American Recovery and Reinvestment Act, better known as the stimulus, certainly helped the working and middle class. The stimulus social spending—like the child care money and the TANF [Temporary Assistance for Needy Families] Emergency Contingency Fund, which created a job subsidy program for parents receiving welfare—made palpable differences in people's lives. The stimulus both created and saved jobs in New York City—some 22,000 in the third quarter of 2010 alone—and unemployment would have risen without it.

Yet the stimulus didn't do nearly enough: It wasn't big enough, direct enough or targeted enough to help the people who needed it most. In New York, as in much of the country, those who needed it most have tended to be the young, people of color, and low-income and blue-collar workers. They are women like Luz Villanueva and Belgica Malu, who stood shivering in yet another job fair line in November, hoping to end their yearlong job search. And they are women like Nancy, a 56-year-old domestic worker from Colombia whose age and limited English and education have conspired to keep her jobless for more than two years. Nearly one in four low-income Latinos reports losing a job or having hours or income reduced, according to the Community Service Society's 2010 "Unheard Third" study, and these women certainly proved the point. Luz and Nancy can barely afford the subway.

They are also men like Chang Ahn, 62, a Korean immigrant with legs made spindly by polio, who lost his job in the classified department of the *Korea Times* in December 2008—a

Economic Indicators for Homelessness

In recognition of the reality that homelessness is most often caused by job loss and other economic factors, this report [by the Homeless Research Institute and National Alliance to End Homelessness] explores economic indicators for homeless people and people at risk of homelessness. The economic indicators examined in this report point to worsening conditions across the nation and all states.

- Conditions worsened among all four economic indicators examined in this report: housing affordability for poor people, unemployment, poor workers' income, and foreclosure status.

- From 2008 to 2009, the number of unemployed people in America increased by 60 percent from 8.9 to 14.3 million. . . .

- Nearly three-quarters of all U.S. households with incomes below the federal poverty line spend over 50 percent of monthly household income on rent. . . .

- While real income among all U.S. workers decreased by 1 percent in 2009, poor workers' income decreased even more, dropping by 2 percent to $9,151. Poor workers in Alaska, the District of Columbia, Maine, and Rhode Island saw their incomes decrease by more than 10 percent.

- Foreclosure affected nearly half a million more households in 2009 than in 2008, a 21 percent increase for a total of 2.8 million foreclosed units in 2009. . . .

M. William Sermons and Peter Witte,
State of Homelessness in America.
Washington, DC: Homeless Research Institute/
National Alliance to End Homelessness, 2011.

job he'd held for twenty years—and has been unable to find work since. He tried to find another media job and even asked fellow church members about washing feet at nail salons, to no avail. He blames his disability and age—and he's probably right; in 2009 men between 55 and 64 held the record for long-term unemployment in New York City, with an average of thirty-nine weeks.

Homeless for the First Time

And then there is David Ward, a 24-year-old father of two, who stood outside the city's intake center for homeless families on a chilly November day, preparing to enter the homeless system for the first time. "I never expected to come here—never wanted to—I always expected to do things on my own, with a job," he says. But after failing to find work more than two years after losing his job at Rite Aid, he finds himself shoved toward an unexpected bitter reality. In this reality, young men with limited education and even more limited means can spend years trying to find a job, with no luck. In this reality, only one in four black men in New York City between 16 and 24 is employed, as a recent study by the Community Service Society reveals. And in this reality, the jobs that were created by the stimulus, many through infrastructure projects, went largely to people with more skills, education, work experience and access.

A targeted approach to job creation—in the form of affirmative action hiring, direct job creation or wage subsidies for companies that hire particular groups of workers—would have helped moderate this trend. But for the most part that didn't happen. The stimulus money was simply released, with little direction and even less accountability.

"I think the administration was very reluctant to create targeted programs," says the Women of Color Policy Network's Mason. "But you cannot just ignore [these communities] and say, 'Well, everything will work itself out.' This is the same problem with the trickle-down economics," she continues. "If I have a broken leg and you have a small cut on your finger, it doesn't make sense to put a patch on both those things. They're different remedies, and they call for different types of responses."

And there's another problem. Some of the most effective stimulus programs were either too narrow in scope or too poorly funded to make the difference they could have. The summer youth employment program is one example. An enormously useful way to introduce young people into the workforce, this program provided jobs and training to more than 35,000 young New Yorkers during the summer of 2010. But it was not funded adequately enough to meet the full need, and its three-month time limit undercut its purpose. "The summer program by itself is not enough to change people's lives," says Sum. "You've got to do year-round job creation."

More distressing is the case of the TANF Emergency Contingency Fund. This program created some 240,000 jobs nationwide for low-income parents receiving welfare and was considered so effective that even some Republicans were gaga for it. So what happened? Congress let its funding lapse on September 30—leaving people like Pamela Brown, the former Bank of America assistant, stuck cleaning streets for the welfare department. "They've never looked at my résumé," she says.

As Goes New York, So Goes the Nation

Outside the precincts of New York, the story is not much cheerier. As Andrew Sum and Ishwar Khatiwada's study demonstrates, nationwide, suffering during the recession followed a straight Euclidean line from poorest to richest, with the poorest enduring catastrophic job losses, those in the middle enduring significant though less pervasive job losses and the richest enjoying scarcely a blip. Or put differently, New York is a near perfect allegory for the cruel geometry of this recession.

A glance at more recent unemployment data that Sum and Khatiwada updated for the *Nation* tells the story. Between January and October 2010, average unemployment rates for workers in the lowest income decile (those with a household income of $12,499 or less) hovered at 29.4 percent, a figure that surpasses the Great Depression's nationwide unemployment high of 25 percent. For those in the second-lowest income decile ($12,500 to $19,999), unemployment hovered at 20.1 percent. Among those in the third-lowest ($20,000 to $29,999), it was 14.9 percent—and on and on in an increasingly cheerful progression to those in the top two deciles ($100,000 to $149,999 and $150,000 and above), who enjoyed the impressively low unemployment rates of 4.1 and 3.4 percent respectively. "See those last two groups?" asks Sum. "We call that full employment."

Sum and Khatiwada did similar analyses for underemployment rates and underutilization rates (a figure that combines the unemployed, the underemployed and those who are not looking but still want work). In each instance the data follow the same distressing pyramid pattern. Underemployed workers in the bottom decile were working part time or at reduced hours at almost ten times the rate of those in the top decile, or 19.5 percent compared with 2 percent. Underutilized workers in the bottom decile were "underutilized" at roughly seven times the rate of those in the top income decile (and two and a half to three times the rate for their own group in the 1990s). Which is to say: While 49 percent (or one out of every two) of the poorest Americans were "underutilized" during the first ten months of 2010, only 6.8 percent of those in the top income decile shared this fate. Overall, nearly 30 million workers were "underutilized."

Worse than the Third World

"This [disparity] is worse than the worst Third World country I've ever seen in my life," says Sum. "And nobody wants to openly admit this because they want this little myth that we're all in this together—the jobless is everybody. No, it is not. It is overwhelmingly among low income and then low-middle income."

For Sum, the solution to this skew is at once obvious and challenging. At its most basic, it primarily requires good old-fashioned, WPA [Works Progress Administration]-style job creation, particularly for young people, the group hit hardest by the recession. "I would take all the stimulus money and put it directly into job creation," he says. But in an important twist on what the government did the last time around, this stimulus would be "very targeted." There would be guidelines requiring any company or agency that gets stimulus money to hire real people—not just stash the money away in their budgets, as so many did—and to hire unemployed people more specifically. Moreover, there would be incentives, in the form of wage subsidies and tax credits, to induce companies to hire low-income workers, young and adult. And there would be training and education. Call it a trickle-up recovery.

But how does any of this happen now? In the wake of Republican victories, it's hard to imagine that we're in for a change in policy anytime soon. And yet there are faint stirrings of hope: in the coalitions of the unemployed; the 99er unions; the grassroots groups that have come together to fight for job creation, unemployment insurance, TANF funding and more. They have not given up.

Pamela Brown was never an activist during her years in the banking trenches, but unemployment and welfare have made her a self-described dissident. In 2009 she joined Community Voices Heard, a grassroots group of low-income New Yorkers, and became a leader in its fight for jobs and welfare rights. "The only way we're going to change our lives collectively is to get politically engaged," she says. "It's that simple."

Periodical and Internet Sources Bibliography

The following articles have been selected to supplement the diverse views presented in this chapter.

David Abel — "Panhandlers Move from Street to Internet: Online Sites Offer a Fertile Venue for Some in Need," *Boston Globe*, October 26, 2009.

Esmeralda Bermudez — "Made Homeless by Tornado, Alabama Victims Ponder Their Next Moves," *Los Angeles Times*, April 30, 2011.

Gustavo Capdevila — "Human Rights: More than 100 Million Homeless Worldwide," Inter Press Service, March 30, 2005. www.ipsnews.net.

Ernest Dempsey — "Around 1.5 Million Homeless as US Enters 2011," *Digital Journal*, December 30, 2010. http://digitaljournal.com.

Eugenia Didenko and Nicole Pankratz — "Substance Use: Pathways to Homelessness? Or a Way of Adapting to Street Life?," *Visions: BC's Mental Health and Addictions Journal*, vol. 4, no. 1, 2007.

Steven Gray — "Report Says 1 in 50 US Kids Is Homeless," *Time*, March 10, 2009. www.time.com.

Rick Jervis — "Homeless Still Feel Katrina's Wrath," *USA Today*, March 17, 2008. www.usatoday.com.

Robert Karash — "Who Is Homeless? The HUD Annual Report to Congress and Homelessness Pulse Project," *Spare Change News* (Boston), June 18, 2010. http://sparechangenews.net.

National Mental Health Association — "Ending Homelessness for People with Mental Illnesses and Co-Occurring Disorders," April 2006.

CHAPTER 3

What Housing Policies Will Benefit the Homeless?

Chapter Preface

As some of the authors in this chapter discuss, many cities nationwide have effectively criminalized homelessness by adopting "quality-of-life" laws that make it illegal to do such things as sleep outdoors, sit on a sidewalk, or ask a stranger for spare change. The reasoning is that such activities negatively affect the quality of life of the community as a whole. Business merchants in particular are sensitive to the presence of homeless people near their shops because they believe they drive away business and make shoppers feel uncomfortable; merchants often spearhead the push for quality-of-life and anti-panhandling ordinances in their cities in the belief that such restrictions will make the homeless less obtrusive in public spaces.

But many cities are taking the criminalization of homelessness a step further by also making it illegal for private individuals or groups to help homeless people by giving them free food. In the summer of 2011 alone, more than twenty members of the nonprofit group Food Not Bombs were arrested in Orlando, Florida, for serving free meals to homeless people in a city park. Members of the all-volunteer group, which has served free vegetarian meals in more than a thousand cities worldwide since 1980, continue to challenge the homeless feeding ban and face arrest in Orlando and elsewhere around the country. Houston, Atlanta, Las Vegas, Denver, Cincinnati, Nashville, Phoenix, Portland, San Diego, and San Francisco are just a few of the other cities where similar meal bans have been enacted. In some places, it is even illegal to simply hand someone a sandwich or to leave a carton of restaurant leftovers on the street so it can be found by a homeless person, a common practice in many urban areas.

Those who oppose free public meals complain that the organized feedings often draw crowds of a hundred or more homeless people, who are highly visible as they loiter in the area and commit offenses such as illegal camping, consuming alcohol, and urinating in public. They believe that free public feedings actually attract homeless people to the area who would otherwise not be there and that it encourages them to congregate. Those who support feeding bans believe that free meals help enable homelessness and that homeless people will be more likely to seek and accept formal help from a city shelter or charity if they do not have easy access to free food.

While Orlando mayor Buddy Dyer has publicly called Food Not Bombs volunteers "food terrorists" for their persistent efforts to feed the homeless in his city, those who serve up the free meals maintain that sharing food is a simple but powerful gesture of hope and humanity in a society where those things are in short supply, especially for people experiencing homelessness. The authors in this chapter present differing viewpoints regarding what practices and policies benefit homeless people most directly.

| *"The right to housing framework gives us a tool for holding the government accountable."*

Housing Must Be Viewed as a Human Right

National Law Center on Homelessness & Poverty

In the following viewpoint, the National Law Center on Homelessness & Poverty (NLCHP) asserts that the United States falls short in its legal and moral obligation to meet international standards that designate housing as a human right. Even though the United States signed the Universal Declaration of Human Rights, put forth by the United Nations General Assembly in 1948, the NLCHP argues here that the country has since fallen behind the rest of the world in the way it views the right to housing. As the legal arm of the nationwide movement to end homelessness, the NLCHP uses litigation, policy advocacy, and public education to bring about change, and in this viewpoint it urges the United States to "bring international language back home" as a foundation for public debate and housing policies and programs.

As you read, consider the following questions:

1. In the opinion of the NLCHP, what does the government have ultimate responsibility for if it is not expected to simply provide free housing for those who need it?

2. If international standards were incorporated into American domestic policies, what does the author believe the result would be?

3. In the NLCHP's opinion, what should the US Senate do in regard to the International Covenant on Economic, Social and Cultural Rights (ICESCR)?

In 1944, Franklin Roosevelt declared that the U.S. had adopted a "second Bill of Rights," including the right to a decent home. The U.S. signed the Universal Declaration of Human Rights in 1948, recognizing housing as a human right. Since that time, the concept of the right to housing has been further developed at the international level. However, the U.S. has fallen behind the rest of the world in making this right a reality. France, Scotland, South Africa and Ecuador have adopted the right to housing in their constitutions or legislation, leading to improved housing conditions. Recent polling indicates that over 50% of Americans strongly believe that adequate housing is a human right, and 2/3 believe that government programs may need to be expanded to ensure this right. Nevertheless, government policies have not traditionally treated housing as a right, and thus the housing needs of the most vulnerable Americans have gone unfulfilled. U.S. housing advocates can and should use international human rights standards to reframe public debate, craft and support legislative proposals, supplement legal claims in court, advocate in international fora and support community organizing efforts.

In the human rights framework, every right creates a corresponding duty on the part of the government to respect, protect, and fulfill the right. In the U.S., we value the right to a fair trial in criminal proceedings, so for those who cannot afford one, the government pays for a lawyer. Having the right to housing does not mean that the government must build a house for every person in America and give it to them free of charge. It does, however, allocate ultimate responsibility to the government for ensuring all people have access to adequate housing.

The Right to Housing Framework

The human right to housing consists of seven elements: Security of Tenure; Availability of Services, Materials, and Infrastructure; Affordability; Accessibility; Habitability; Location; and Cultural Adequacy. The government can choose how it will implement the right, whether through spending on public housing and voucher programs; by creating incentives for private development of affordable housing such as inclusionary zoning or the Low-Income Housing Tax Credit; through market regulation such as rent control; through legal due process protections from eviction or foreclosure; or by other means. The right to housing framework gives us a tool for holding the government accountable if not all those elements are satisfied.

The right to housing has been developed through a number of international treaties and other documents, many of which were signed or otherwise affirmed by the U.S. First included in the Universal Declaration of Human Rights in 1948, the right was codified in the International Covenant on Economic, Social and Cultural Rights (ICESCR) in 1966. The U.S. has signed, but not ratified the ICESCR, and thus is not strictly bound to uphold the right to housing as framed in that document. However, the U.S. has ratified the International Convention on the Elimination of All Forms of Racial Discrimination (ICERD) and the International Covenant on Civil and Political Rights (ICCPR), both of which recognize the right to nondiscrimination on the basis of race or other status, including in housing. Additional standards can be found in other documents such as the Habitat Declaration or the UN [United Nations] Basic Principles [and Guidelines] on Development-Based Evictions [and Displacement]. Many of these standards have language that, if incorporated into domestic policies, would significantly improve on existing U.S. policies, and U.S. advocates could learn much from them.

Using Human Rights in the United States

U.S. groups are using international mechanisms to promote housing rights. In 2006, the U.N. Human Rights Committee reviewed the U.S. for compliance with the ICCPR. Following advocacy by NLCHP [National Law Center on Homelessness & Poverty] and others, the committee, in its final report, expressed concern about the disparate racial impact of homelessness and ordered the U.S. to pursue "adequate and adequately implemented policies to ensure the cessation of this form of de facto and historically generated racial discrimination." In 2008, a similar review by the Committee on the Elimination of Racial Discrimination under the ICERD resulted in a number of observations concerning the right to housing, including segregation in housing, affordable housing planning, the right to civil counsel in housing court, lack of domestic violence shelters on Native American land, and the right to return for victims of Hurricane Katrina.

Bringing this international language back home, advocates in Minneapolis used the ICCPR and ICERD comments in pushing for the repeal of an "anti-lurking" ordinance, which was having a discriminatory impact on homeless and minority residents. Advocates also used the May 2008 visit of the U.N. Special Rapporteur on Racism to put an international spotlight on the ordinance. Although the motion to repeal the ordinance ultimately failed by one vote, the public pressure forced the police department to meet with advocates and reduced the harmful enforcement of the ordinance.

United Nations Universal Declaration of Human Rights

Adopted December 10, 1948, by the General Assembly of the United Nations (without dissent)

The General Assembly proclaims this Universal Declaration of Human Rights as a common standard of achievement for all peoples and all nations, to the end that every individual and every organ of society, keeping this Declaration constantly in mind, shall strive by teaching and education to promote respect for these rights and freedoms and by progressive measures, national and international, to secure their universal and effective recognition and observance, both among the peoples of Member States themselves and among the peoples of territories under their jurisdiction. . . .

Article 25

(1) Everyone has the right to a standard of living adequate for the health and well-being of himself and of his family, including food, clothing, housing and medical care and necessary social services, and the right to security in the event of unemployment, sickness, disability, widowhood, old age or other lack of livelihood in circumstances beyond his control.

General Assembly of the United Nations,
Universal Declaration of Human Rights,
G.A. resolution 217A (III), U.N. Doc A/810 at 71 (1948).

The Scotland Example

Scotland provides us with a good example of the difference the right to housing approach can make. The Homeless Etc. (Scotland) Act of 2003 includes the right to be immediately housed for all homeless persons and the right to long-term, supportive housing as long as is needed for priority groups—a category that will be progressively abolished by 2012 at which point the right will extend to all. This includes particularly at-risk groups, such as former prisoners, who are excluded from much housing assistance in the U.S. Crucially, this includes an individual right to sue if one believes these rights are not being met. Complementary policies include a number of other rights, including the right to purchase public housing units and automatic referrals by banks to foreclosure prevention programs to help people remain in their homes. All these elements work together to ensure the right to housing is upheld.

Revitalizing the Right to Housing

Advocates are working with Rep. [Maxine] Waters' office to hold congressional field hearings on the crisis in affordable housing in the spring of 2009 in several cities across the country, explicitly framing housing as a human right. Rep. Waters will introduce a resolution calling for a right to housing for children. Additional legislation, from the Protecting Tenants at Foreclosure Act of 2009 to funding the National Housing Trust Fund, will be advanced as steps toward realizing a right to housing. The Senate should pass the ICESCR as a basis for grounding economic recovery efforts in a rights-based framework.

> *"Housing vouchers enable families to af-*
> *ford decent housing by paying the dif-*
> *ference between the cost of a modest*
> *rental unit and 30 percent of a family's*
> *income."*

Government Housing Vouchers Help Homeless Families Best

Barbara Sard

According to housing voucher expert Barbara Sard, a growing number of American families are living at or below the poverty line. In the following viewpoint, Sard explains how the recent economic recession has increased their risk of homelessness because of widespread home foreclosures and foreclosure-driven displacements from rental units. Federal housing vouchers, argues Sard, are effective in preventing homelessness and should be made a funding priority in any governmental stimulus or economic recovery funding package. Sard maintains that it is essential to increase such housing assistance in times of economic hardship. Sard is the vice president for housing policy at the

Center on Budget and Policy Priorities, a Washington, DC–based organization that works to address fiscal policy and public programs for low- and moderate-income individuals.

As you read, consider the following questions:

1. According to the author, what families are at the greatest risk of becoming homeless?

2. What two things does the author say are exacerbating the risks of homelessness?

3. What situations does Jill Khadduri say a family will likely avoid if given a housing voucher?

In the next few years [from 2009], the nation is likely to experience the sharpest increases in severe poverty in over 30 years. During the last three recessions, the number of Americans living in poverty—as well as the number living below *half* of the poverty line, a commonly used measure of "deep" or "severe" poverty—has risen markedly, with the largest increases occurring in recessions with the highest unemployment. Based on the relationship between increases in the unemployment rate and increases in poverty in the past three recessions, the number of severely poor families with children—that is, the number living below *half* of the poverty line—is expected to rise by 900,000—1.1 million as a result of the current economic downturn.

Families with incomes below half of the poverty line are at the greatest risk of becoming homeless. Not surprisingly, these families have the most difficulty paying rent. A family of four with income at half of the poverty line has a monthly income of $833, or less than the $900 average cost of a modest two-bedroom apartment. Families that lose their housing may be able to "double up" temporarily with relatives or friends, but such arrangements often do not last.

Moreover, very poor families may be at greater risk of homelessness in this recession than in previous recessions because the safety net to protect jobless families against destitution is now weaker than it was during previous major recessions. . . .

Turmoil in the Housing Sector Exacerbates Risks of Homelessness

The current severe problems in the housing sector and the growing number of foreclosures are exacerbating the risks of homelessness. Both homeowners and renters are being displaced into the rental housing market as an increasing number of owners become subject to foreclosure or walk away from "underwater" mortgages. National data indicate that at least 20 percent of foreclosed properties are *not* owner-occupied, and in many parts of the country (such as New England, New York City, and Minneapolis), half or more of households living in foreclosed buildings are renters.

When foreclosure occurs, renters usually are forced to vacate, even if they have not missed any rent payments and regardless of whether they have access to funds needed for the up-front costs of a new apartment. This is because lenders (such as banks) who foreclose on properties typically are reluctant to act as landlords and consequently evict tenants while they attempt to sell the properties. [Federal lender] Fannie Mae recently announced that it would no longer require renters who are up to date on rental payments to move after foreclosure, but it is not yet clear whether other lenders will make similar changes in their practices voluntarily.

Furthermore, as a result of the troubles in the housing market, many families who previously were owners now are seeking to rent, and many renter families that would otherwise be purchasing homes are waiting for prices (and the economy) to stabilize before doing so. Thus, although home prices are falling, rents have continued to rise in a number of areas due to an increased demand for rental units. In the greater Boston area, for example, the median home price has dropped by 11 percent since 2005 but rents have risen 12 percent, the result of a decrease in vacancy rates for rental units as foreclosed homeowners move into rental housing and fewer renters move into homeownership.

These developments come at an inopportune time. The number of poor renter families with severe housing affordability problems (i.e., who pay at least half of their income for housing) was rising markedly even before the current economic downturn; it increased 29 percent from 2001 to 2007. It will rise further as the economy contracts.

Family Homelessness Is Increasing in Many Areas

Before the recession began, HUD [the US Department of Housing and Urban Development] reported that there were 131,000 homeless families with children residing in emergency shelters or transitional housing facilities (other than shelters that serve victims of domestic violence) during the year ending September 30, 2007. HUD also reported that communities counted 51,000 homeless families with children who were on the streets or in cars, abandoned buildings, or other places not fit for habitation during the January 2007 "point in time" count of homeless people. As many as several hundred thousand additional families with children apparently had no place of their own to live and were living temporarily with others; in the 2006–2007 school year, public schools reported 680,000 homeless children, some of whom were literally homeless (and thus likely to be reflected in the HUD data), and others of whom were doubled up in what were often unstable living arrangements. . . .

The surveys of cities and school districts indicate that the weakening of the economy is helping to drive the increase in homeless families. A majority of the cities reporting in the recent Conference of Mayors survey also attributed part of the recent increase in homelessness to foreclosures. Similarly, about half of the school districts responding to the recent survey reported an increase in homeless children due to the economic downturn, and 29 percent reported an increase due to foreclosures. . . .

If public policies do not prevent a large increase in homeless children in this recession, the adverse consequences for some children could be long-lasting. Various studies have found that housing instability and homelessness lower academic performance, increase the chances of repeating a grade, and reduce high school completion rates. One study found that children experiencing homelessness are almost three times as likely as other children to suffer from emotional or behavioral problems that interfere with learning. Homelessness is also associated with children being at greater risk of severe physical health problems than other similarly poor children.

The specific causal pathways connecting housing instability and learning are not well understood; researchers hypothesize that disruptions in courses of instruction or in social networks that reinforce learning, as well as the stress and anxiety caused by the underlying economic hardships, may be responsible for the increased educational difficulties that children in unstable homes experience. It seems clear, however, that frequent moves and school changes set children back in ways that may endure even after housing stabilizes.

Housing Vouchers Effectively Prevent Homelessness

Some families at risk of homelessness due to the downturn could avert homelessness if they secured help paying a few months of overdue rent or utility bills or meeting the costs of moving into a new apartment. Relocation funds could be particularly effective in helping families meet the one-time costs associated with getting settled in new housing after being displaced by foreclosure.

How Federal Housing Vouchers Work

The housing choice voucher program is the federal government's major program for assisting very low-income families, the elderly, and the disabled to afford decent, safe, and sanitary housing in the private market. Since housing assistance is provided on behalf of the family or individual, participants are able to find their own housing, including single-family homes, townhouses and apartments.

The participant is free to choose any housing that meets the requirements of the program and is not limited to units located in subsidized housing projects.

Housing choice vouchers are administered locally by public housing agencies (PHAs). The PHAs receive federal funds from the US Department of Housing and Urban Development (HUD) to administer the voucher program.

A family that is issued a housing voucher is responsible for finding a suitable housing unit of the family's choice where the owner agrees to rent under the program. . . .

A housing subsidy is paid to the landlord directly by the PHA on behalf of the participating family. The family then pays the difference between the actual rent charged by the landlord and the amount subsidized by the program. . . .

Eligibility for a housing voucher is determined by the PHA based on the total annual gross income and family size and is limited to US citizens and specified categories of non-citizens who have eligible immigration status. In general, the family's income may not exceed 50% of the median income for the county or metropolitan area in which the family chooses to live.

US Department of Housing and Urban Development,
"Housing Choice Vouchers Fact Sheet," January 2011.
www.hud.gov.

Currently, the federal government funds homelessness prevention activities through two funding streams: the Emergency Food and Shelter Program (EFSP, administered by the United Way, with a federally appointed board of nonprofit organizations) and the Emergency Shelter Grant (ESG) program administered by HUD. EFSP received a significant funding increase for 2009 as part of the Homeland Security bill, and the network of agencies through which it works is unlikely to be able to expand further in the time frame needed.

ESG, by contrast (which allocates funds to states and the same local jurisdictions that receive entitlement funding under the Community Development Block Grant [CDBG] program, using the CDBG formula), could productively use more funds. A significant increase in funding for ESG homelessness prevention activities would be an efficient and cost-effective strategy. State and local administrators could effectively use substantially more homelessness prevention funding by working with large networks of existing service providers that form the front line of communities' strategies for responding to homelessness.

For such short-term assistance to be most effective, however, families must be able to sustain their ongoing rental costs. If a parent is unable to find a full-time, steady job and does not qualify for unemployment insurance or another program that provides sufficient income maintenance, very short-term housing assistance could be a "bridge to nowhere." Even if the forthcoming economic recovery legislation includes measures to temporarily increase food stamp benefits and unemployment insurance (in addition to initiatives to generate additional jobs), a substantial increase in the number of very poor families is virtually certain to occur, given the steep increase in unemployment that is anticipated.

Vouchers and Economic Recovery

It therefore makes sense also to include a substantial number of additional housing vouchers in the economic recovery package. Housing vouchers enable families to afford decent housing by paying the difference between the cost of a modest rental unit and 30 percent of a family's income (after certain deductions). Because the amount of the subsidy adjusts with changes in family income, the voucher program works well in an economic downturn, and costs decline as participants become employed and increase their earnings.

Recent evidence from a rigorous, five-year study confirms what previous research indicated: Housing vouchers are effective in preventing homelessness. The federally funded Voucher Family Study found that voucher assistance resulted in a 74 percent decrease in the incidence of "official" homelessness. That is, control group members—similarly poor families that did not receive housing vouchers—were four times more likely to have resided in a shelter or on the streets in the fourth year of the study than comparable families that were provided vouchers and rented housing with them.

Reviewing these and other findings, noted researcher and former HUD policy director Jill Khadduri has written:

> An extensive body of careful research has demonstrated that housing vouchers are critically important both for preventing families with children from becoming homeless and for helping those who do enter the shelter system to leave it for permanent housing and not become homeless again. . . . [H]aving a voucher serves as protection against the pattern of housing instability that can lead to homelessness; having a voucher virtually eliminates the risk that the family will enter a shelter or sleep in a place not fit for human habitation. For families who do become homeless, housing vouchers are an extensively tested and demonstrably effective tool for moving to permanent housing and remaining stably housed.

Vouchers Are Not an Entitlement

Federal housing assistance serves only about one of every four eligible low-income households. Unlike most other major components of the safety net, housing assistance is not an entitlement; appropriations bills and other policies limit the number of families that can be served. And while some families leave the programs each year, freeing up resources for new applicants, fewer families are likely to become independent of federal housing assistance during an economic downturn, which means that fewer new families can be assisted now than would usually be the case.

In 2008, for the first time in six years, Congress provided funding for a small number of additional households to receive housing assistance. But few of the roughly 15,000 new housing vouchers will be available to homeless (or imminently homeless) families with children; most of the vouchers are set aside for people with disabilities or homeless veterans. Only approximately 2,840 of the new vouchers can be used for families with children, and these families must be connected to the foster care system.

It is unlikely that the 2009 appropriations bill will provide more than a similarly small number of new vouchers for families with children. The Senate version of the bill would provide about the same number of new vouchers for families with children in the foster care system as in 2008, plus another 10,000 new vouchers for homeless veterans. The House bill would provide about 14,000 new vouchers, all for people with disabilities or homeless veterans. Congress is expected to finalize the 2009 appropriations for HUD and other agencies early in 2009.

Only a small number of new families with children thus will be able to receive voucher assistance in 2009 unless Congress includes funding for additional vouchers in the economic recovery package. It is reasonable to expect that state and local housing agencies could serve about 10 percent more households in 2009 than in 2008, if they received the requisite resources. This suggests including funding for 200,000 additional vouchers in the recovery package. . . .

Immediate and Long-Term Benefits

In addition to the immediate and long-term benefits of preventing homelessness and ensuring housing stability, the new vouchers would begin to inject funds into local economies within four to six months after enactment, with an impact on the weak housing sector. And families receiving vouchers that currently are spending most of their income on rent would be able to spend more on food, clothing, health care, and other necessities, boosting total household consumption.

Current evidence leaves little doubt that the worsening recession will cause a substantial increase in homelessness, particularly among families with children. The harm that housing instability and homelessness can inflict on children is significant. To the extent that we can avoid this harm, it is important that a comprehensive package to address the recession include measures to do so.

Housing vouchers are a proven and effective tool to prevent homelessness. The existing administrative infrastructure could quickly provide vouchers to about 200,000 additional households. Homelessness among hundreds of thousands of additional families, including those displaced by foreclosures, can potentially be averted by short-term rental or relocation assistance through HUD's Emergency Shelter Grant program.

Together the cost of these two measures would be about one-half of one percent of the total recovery package. While the level of expenditure would be modest, it would have a major impact on homelessness and destitution. It also would provide some stimulus through the infusion of funds into local economies.

> *"By combating the lack of emergency housing for children and families and instituting programs to help get them off the streets, we inherently improve the quality of life for all members of our community."*

Effective Emergency Shelters Help Homeless Families Best

Thomas Almeida and Kyra Bando, et al.

In the fall of 2010, students in a class called Action Research Seminar at the University of Illinois at Urbana-Champaign conducted research about how best to assist homeless families in the city of Champaign. Their findings are presented in the following viewpoint, which details the unique complications of sheltering families, the different types of shelter options available to various family groups, and the special impacts of homelessness on children. The authors selected two family shelters in cities similar to their own—Evansville, Indiana, and Ithaca, New York—and they examined the pros and cons of each to identify "critical fac-

Thomas Almeida and Kyra Bando, et al., "Community-Driven Homelessness Housing Programs: Best Practices Report," *Action Research Seminar*, Fall 2010. www.eslarp .uiuc.edu. Copyright © 2010 by Action Research Seminar (University of Illinois at Urbana-Champaign). All rights reserved. Reproduced by permission.

*tors" that contribute to successful family shelter programs. The
authors present them here as case studies on which new programs could be modeled.*

As you read, consider the following questions:

1. Which types of families does the Ozanam Family Shelter
   accommodate?

2. Identify two sources of funding for the Ozanam Family
   Shelter.

3. According to the viewpoint, whom does the Red Cross
   Emergency Shelter screening process target?

In a time of crisis, families can be our biggest support system. However, the City of Champaign [Illinois] has never
had a facility that can accommodate homeless families as an
intact unit. In the City of Champaign, 12.8% of all families
live below the poverty line, according to the American Community Survey conducted in 2009. In the midst of a distressed
housing market and a plummeting economy, many low-
income families in Champaign are faced with homelessness,
jeopardizing parents and children alike. The point in time survey counted 594 homeless persons in Champaign County just
last year [2009]. Of these 594 homeless people, 358 were children. That signifies that 67% of Champaign County's homeless population is children. Furthermore, according to the City
of Champaign's Consolidated Plan, the city itself lacks 70
shelter beds for homeless persons in families with children.

Emergency family shelters are complicated because of the
specific population they are addressing. There are many different types of families and therefore many different types of
family shelters. Some emergency family shelters only serve intact families—defined as couples who are married. Other shelters only serve families with children. Some shelters will serve
single parents of both genders. It is often the case that emergency family shelters will also serve single women. Sometimes,

emergency family shelters will not accommodate single men, and if geared specifically for women with children, these shelters frequently cannot assist males in their teens, meaning women with male children may be turned away from the shelter. This is the case for Champaign's Center for Women in Transition. In the City of Champaign, intact families must split up in order to be accommodated by our current continuum of housing.

There are some families that experience chronic homelessness, but even more families will experience a temporary crisis. The top reasons that a family would experience a temporary crisis include: fires, divorce, layoffs and abuse. Families that are temporarily homeless typically stay about thirty days in an emergency shelter.

Children and Homelessness

We cannot underestimate the harmful impact that homelessness can have on children and families. HUD's [the US Department of Housing and Urban Development's] study on Homeless Families and Children examines this impact (2009). It explains that homelessness has a negative effect on mental health and behavior, creates education-related problems, stunts development and also causes health complications. In short-term studies, the effects ranged between mild and moderate degrees of intensity. However, low-income children fared worse overall than children in the general population on a variety of tests. Although the complexities of emergency family shelters make them a challenging project to develop, it is crucial that the community move forward on this much-needed service. By combating the lack of emergency housing for children and families and instituting programs to help get them off the streets, we inherently improve the quality of life for all members of our community.

In the rest of this section of our report, we will be examining cities similar to Champaign that have developed successful emergency family housing projects. We will be assessing the successes and any setbacks or shortcomings of these projects. We will ultimately develop a sense of the critical factors that contribute to the success of an emergency family shelter based on the examples we have studied. Finally, we will compile a list of recommendations that the City of Champaign could use as a framework for a potential project. We have focused on two specific case studies, the Ozanam Family Shelter in Evansville, IN, and the Red Cross Shelter in Ithaca, NY. We will combine attributes from these two shelters and learn from their city government's involvement.

Case Study: Ozanam Family Shelter, Evansville, IN

One particular city that is strikingly similar to Champaign is Evansville, IN. According to the 2006–2008 American Community Survey, Evansville had an approximate population of 113,551 persons. Champaign, according to the same survey, had a population of 78,174. Evansville is comparable to Champaign for a number of reasons. First, Evansville is also a college town. It is home to two different universities, the University of Southern Indiana, as well as the University of Evansville. They also have a community college similar in size to Parkland. The median household incomes of the two cities are also extremely close. Champaign's median household income was $38,860. Evansville's median household income was $34,629. The most important similarity, for the purpose of this report, is the percent of families living under the poverty level. In Evansville, 13.7% of families live under the poverty level, while in Champaign, 12.8% of families live under the poverty level. These percentages reflect the fact that Evansville's need for emergency family housing is comparable to Champaign's need.

Evansville has been home to the very successful Ozanam Family Shelter for over a decade. In this shelter, families are provided three meals a day as well as individual case managers that help get them back on their feet. There are no time limits placed on the stay, but the average stay is about 38 days. During their stay families are encouraged, but not required, to participate in certain programs. These programs include life skills workshops, job assistance counseling, parenting classes, activities for children, help with school work and referrals for medical and psychiatric assistance.

The shelter accommodates intact families, couples with children, single fathers and single mothers. They are one of the only shelters in the area that can accommodate men. There is another shelter in their Continuum of Care called House of Bread and Peace that accommodates women and children. Also, their local YMCA has beds for single women. Ozanam is the only one among them that will take in intact families. Ozanam has eighteen total rooms—seventeen of the rooms are family rooms that are capable of housing between two and nine family members. The eighteenth room is used to house up to six single women. Rooms are designed to look like "homes," with furniture such as bunk beds, cribs, desks, dressers. The families all share common areas including living rooms, reading/recreation rooms, laundry facilities and a community kitchen. Families come to the shelter and are matched with rooms that best fit their needs.

Funding Sources

Funding for Ozanam comes from a wide range of sources. Federal and state grants account for 30% of the total costs. The shelter received Community Development Block Grant (CDBG) funding from the state as well as municipal Emergency Shelter Grants for the bricks and mortar and redevelopment. Much of the funding for Ozanam's operations comes from United Way. United Way gets FEMA [Federal Emergency Management Agency] funds and will often match donations from other agencies. The rest of the funding comes from local agencies and individuals. They receive this funding through religious charities, individuals, foundations, businesses and their community partners.

The city government has been instrumental in connecting the different community partners that support Ozanam's efforts. These community partners include, but are not limited to DFC (Drug Free Communities), DSS (Department of Social Services), other local homeless shelters, medical facilities, mental health facilities—including Southwest Indiana Mental Health [Center], religious foundations and other community and social agencies. Many interfaith organizations are also involved in funding. Various churches and church officials have been crucial in filling out Evansville's Continuum of Care by volunteering as well as donating funds. These agencies provide not only funding, but staff support, maintenance and upkeep as well as case management. Purdue University is another important community partner for Evansville. Purdue provides nutrition resources to the shelter. Much of the funding that comes from these various organizations flows through the state. For example, Southwestern Behavioral Healthcare receives funds from the state to work with Ozanam in providing mental health resources.

Management Is Crucial

The shelter is run by a board of directors as well as many administrative staffers and family advocates. The shelter is staffed with House Managers, who help the shelter's day-to-day functions and are there 24/7. The shelter also relies on the help of volunteers from time to time to assist with cleaning, rearranging furniture and other tasks. Gayl Killough, the city's Community Development Specialist, has been an instrumental part of the shelter's success. She is directly involved with the leaders of Evansville's Continuum of Care. She attends many meetings and sub-meetings with different leaders of their shelters. She is well known in the community and connects different agencies together to promote efficiency. Killough explained the importance of city government's involvement, "that's what's good about being at the local level versus the state and federal level. You are right there where it is all happening." She assists with troubleshooting and day-to-day tasks at the Ozanam shelter. Often times, shelters can fall apart without good management. Killough and other city officials are responsible for making sure the management and maintenance of their shelters are up to par. The city regularly meets with agency contacts and directors and has good control over their Continuum of Care. Killough explained this succinctly by telling me, "If they [managers of various shelters] are not doing their job or spending their money right, I'll know about it real quick."

Case Study 2: Red Cross Emergency Shelter, Ithaca, NY

Another location that can be compared to the City of Champaign is Ithaca, New York. Ithaca is located in Tompkins County. Although the City of Ithaca is smaller in population than Champaign (just over 30,000 residents), its other attributes make for a good case study location. Like Champaign, Ithaca is the home of a major university with an enrollment of just over 21,000 students, as well as another smaller college that has an enrollment of over 6,000 students. The demographics in Ithaca are also quite comparable to those of the City of Champaign. Tompkins County is comprised of 72.3% whites, 6.0% African Americans, 15.9% Asian, and a mix of other races. To accommodate homeless families in Ithaca and the surrounding Tomkins County area, they have the Red Cross Emergency Shelter.

The Homeless Services Program at the Red Cross in Ithaca offers a wide range of resources for the homeless in the community. Currently, they have an emergency shelter that offers a place to stay for families, individuals, and runaway youth in the community. The shelter has a fully stocked kitchen, two full bathrooms, laundry facilities, and staff working 24/7. Families that use the shelter's services must adhere to the shelter rules and work with a caseworker from the Department of Social Services (DSS) to get back into a stable home environment. The caseworkers screen potential clients for eligibility based on income levels. This ensures that the families who are seeking help are actually benefitting from the resources provided. The screening process targets the transitionally homeless, rather than those who require a more intensive approach to getting out of homelessness. The shelter building is leased from a nonprofit organization called Community Housing [of] Ithaca, which seeks to provide the local Ithaca community with affordable housing solutions. They play a major role in the success of the Red Cross Emergency Shelter, saving them a considerable sum of money by giving them a place to run their operations at low cost.

Funding Sources

Through the Continuum of Care (CoC) Committee, the Red Cross organization has influence in how funds from the state are divvied up throughout the county. The CoC meets to discuss applications for grants and prioritizes them according to the community's needs. They are supported by the Tompkins County Legislature, the City of Ithaca Common Council, and the Tompkins County United Way, all of whom work with the committee to determine where funding should go. The Red Cross's involvement with the CoC is integral in getting community support for their operations.

Funding comes from a wide range of sources. Surprisingly, the Red Cross provides no funding. Most of the funding comes from the DSS, with whom they have two separate contracts. The DSS compensates the shelter for each bed-night it provides, which averages at approximately $30 per night, per person. They also fund the Friendship Center operations, which provide daytime services, meals, and counseling to anyone that comes in. The DSS is mandated by the State of New York to fund projects that support families and individuals in their time of need. This is a funded mandate under which they can develop projects like this throughout the county. They receive federal Emergency Shelter Grants and Community Development Block Grants to fund different operations and pay for development. To pay for food expenses, the shelter uses funds from the Hunger Prevention [and] Nutrition Assistance Program. The Red Cross also earns income by charging for community education programs, such as swimming lessons, CPR [cardiopulmonary resuscitation] classes, first aid classes, and other related services in the community.

University collaborations also provide the shelters with significant resources. Purdue and Cornell Universities contribute with research on nutrition and mental health in all shelter operations. The Red Cross shelter also has programs at Cornell and Ithaca College to recruit volunteers. The volunteers in these shelters help cut operational costs; the Red Cross shelter saves about $25,000–$30,000 a year just with the help of its volunteers.

Both the Red Cross shelter and the Ozanam Family Shelter have been successful in their own right. They each offer valuable insight and experience that is applicable to our community.

> "The idea is to target the most difficult cases ... and give them apartments without requiring them to get sober, in the hope that having a place to live will help them address their other problems."

Permanent Housing Before Recovery Reduces Chronic Homelessness

Florence Graves and Hadar Sayfan

As journalists Florence Graves and Hadar Sayfan explain in the following viewpoint, a controversial new approach is emerging for dealing with chronically homeless people. "Housing first" programs across the country provide homeless people with free housing right away, without requiring them to get sober, get a job, or deal with mental health or criminal justice issues first. And, as Graves and Sayfan report, it not only appears to work where all else has failed, but it also saves money. This viewpoint provides a thorough overview of the concept of housing first and also ex-

plores some of the political and systemic resistance to this bold and innovative social services paradigm whose goal is not simply managing homelessness but eliminating it.

As you read, consider the following questions:

1. According to the authors, why do housing-first programs have such broad appeal?

2. What did researcher Dennis Culhane discover about chronically homeless people?

3. Why do some homeless advocates not want to see housing-first programs take the place of the shelter system?

At the Latin Academy, a majestic former school built in 1900 near Dorchester's Codman Square, Joe Jeannotte is participating in a social experiment.

Jeannotte lives in a sparsely furnished new two-bedroom apartment. Light streams through large windows, and a burgundy and forest green couch faces a small television. He looks older than his 38 years—gaunt, scruffy, with dark brown hair—and shares the place with his girlfriend, Judy, who asked that her last name not be used. Often, the noise of construction filters in as workers rehab other apartments, but the couple doesn't complain. Not long ago, they were convinced they would never have a place to live at all. When they moved into the new place, at public expense, they had no home and no money, and both had been struggling for years with heroin addiction.

In the past, society's approach to homeless people with chronic health problems such as addiction has been governed by tough love: Stay in treatment, or you don't get the opportunity for publicly supported housing. People who could not confront their addiction, the thinking went, could not handle an apartment.

But a new approach, called "housing first," is gathering momentum. The idea is to target the most difficult cases—the chronically homeless who make up between 10 and 20 percent of the homeless population and spend years cycling between the streets, shelters, jail cells, and emergency rooms—and give them apartments without requiring them to get sober, in the hope that having a place to live will help them address their other problems. More than 150 cities or counties around the country already have programs of some kind or plans to initiate one, and last month [May 2007] the Massachusetts Senate Ways and Means Committee recommended doubling the size of a small pilot program in the state. If the pilot succeeds, proponents say it could force dramatic changes in homeless policy—and a recognition that the current shelter system, built on what they call a punitive moralism, has fundamentally failed.

"Shelters have become the poor houses of the 21st century," said Joe Finn, executive director of the Massachusetts Housing and Shelter Alliance (MHSA), who is administering Home & Healthy for Good, the pilot program.

A Bipartisan Approach

The program's appeal reaches across the ideological landscape. In 1999, a Republican Congress endorsed the concept, requiring that the US Department of Housing and Urban Development [HUD] devote at least a third of its homelessness funding toward putting the chronically homeless and chronically disabled in permanent housing. Cities like San Francisco, Atlanta, and Portland, Oregon, have become proponents after successful tests. The [George W.] Bush administration has also been enthusiastic. In 2002, it hired Philip Mangano, who spent 25 years in Boston as a homeless advocate, to head its homelessness efforts, and he has evangelized widely for the housing-first approach.

Housing-First Outcomes in Denver

In 2006, the Colorado Coalition for the Homeless conducted a cost-benefit analysis of the Denver Housing First Collaborative, which serves one hundred chronically homeless individuals with a housing-first strategy and community treatment program that provides health, mental health, and substance abuse treatment and support services. Comparison figures are for the twenty-four-month period prior to entering the program and the twenty-four-month period after entering the program.

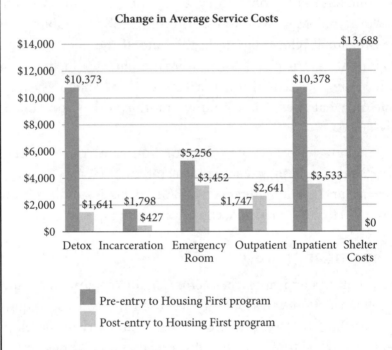

Change in Average Service Costs

Pre-entry to Housing First program
Post-entry to Housing First program

TAKEN FROM: Jennifer Perlman and John Parvensky, "Denver Housing First Collaborative Cost Benefit Analysis and Program Outcomes Report," Colorado Coalition for the Homeless, December 11, 2006. www.coloradocoalition.org.

Part of the program's broad appeal is its counterintuitive claim: that it can often break even or save money while providing housing. Academic studies, based on programs in New

York City and Philadelphia, have found that cities spend almost the same or less money on the housing and other services than they would on shelter beds, emergency rooms, and other health care costs.

"Cost-benefit analysis may be the new compassion," said Mangano, the founding executive director of MHSA. He's now executive director of the federal Interagency Council on Homelessness.

There are also critics across the political spectrum who are uneasy about what they think amounts to rewarding bad behavior—putting drug addicts and alcoholics at the front of the line for housing.

Yet the housing-first movement is part of a broader, more ambitious agenda: ending homelessness, not managing it. Many Americans forget that widespread urban homelessness is a recent problem that began in the early '80s, not an inevitable price of capitalism. For years, a great deal of money has been spent managing homelessness in various ad hoc approaches, particularly shelters.

In pushing the housing-first approach to municipal, county, and state governments, Mangano (and, by extension, the Bush administration) is rejecting the idea that chronic homelessness will always be with us. The problem can be solved, they argue, and, eventually, much of the social-services industry built up around it can and must be dismantled.

It is an argument that longtime advocates say brings a mixture of excitement at the possibilities and fears about what it might mean in practice. Nan Roman, president and CEO [chief executive officer] of the National Alliance to End Homelessness, says some shelter providers have said to her, "If we end homelessness, what are we going to do for a living?"

The Beginnings of "Housing First"

Many observers credit the birth of the housing-first concept to Sam Tsemberis, who calls himself a "recovering psychologist." While treating homeless people for their mental health or substance abuse problems, Tsemberis, who is based in New York City, recognized that "business as usual" was not working. His patients invariably told him that, before they could work on their other problems, they needed housing first. In 1992, he founded Pathways to Housing to provide mentally ill and substance-abusing homeless people with their own apartments immediately.

During the 1990s, Dennis Culhane, a sociology professor at the University of Pennsylvania, started collecting and analyzing the data on all that spending and its effectiveness. In a series of studies, he revealed, among other things, that the chronically homeless population—the mentally ill and addicts who were spending years on the street, in and out of shelters—made up only 10 percent of the homeless population but were using 50 percent of shelter resources. In follow-up studies, he revealed that by focusing on housing this subgroup, communities could better keep down costs and help turn around lives.

A landmark 2002 study by Culhane found that providing housing and other assistance to the homeless could bring down nonhousing expenses almost enough to pay for itself. The study followed mentally ill homeless people between 1989 and 1997 and found that each permanent supported housing unit saved $16,281 a year in public costs for shelter, health care, mental health, and criminal justice, offsetting most of the $17,277 cost of housing and other services.

Mangano, a former seminarian who had focused on housing for the mentally ill in Massachusetts, said he was so impressed by the New York Pathways to Housing program and Culhane's research that he decided to take the ideas and disseminate them nationally.

"[We] committed an act of legitimate larceny," Mangano said.

Medical bills for today's homeless are a large expense. For example, between 1999 and 2003, the Boston Health Care for the Homeless Program (BHCHP), a group that provides primary care for people living on the streets, tracked the medical expenses of 119 chronically homeless clients. All told, the group racked up 18,342 emergency room visits, for an average of more than 36 visits per person each year. At a minimum cost of $1000 a visit, that's an annual emergency room bill of at least $36,000 per person. Lack of stable housing makes it hard for people to rehabilitate after an illness, properly care for wounds, or take medication consistently, according to Dr. Jim O'Connell, the president of BHCHP who headed the study and is also involved in the Home and Healthy for Good pilot in Massachusetts.

By the Numbers

Last year [2006] the state legislature allocated $600,000 for that pilot, which is being tried in locations across Massachusetts. Preliminary data from the program indicate that it is saving the state money, according to MHSA executive director Joe Finn. Home and Healthy for Good has put 155 formerly chronically homeless people into stable housing, paid for their apartments, and assigned them social workers to help them find the services they need. Finn's group concluded that the commonwealth saved, on average, $918 a month during the first six months in shelter and service costs (including health care, hospitalizations, emergency room visits, incarcerations, drug detoxification, and shelters) for each person housed. That's a projected annual savings of $11,016 per person. Federal figures suggest that there are at least 3,137 chronically homeless adults in the state.

The savings are impressive, but some worry they may be inflated. Jim Greene, who heads the city of Boston's Emergency Shelter Commission, suspects that some of the success stories from around the country are misleading, worrying that the people who ran the studies were selective about who they enrolled. But the Massachusetts program has specifically asked for the neediest and most challenging street people, according to Dr. Jessie Gaeta, an MHSA Physician Advocacy Fellow and a clinician for the Boston Health Care for the Homeless Program who is one of the study's investigators. Still, she said, she will not consider any of the results to be valid until they have at least a year's worth of data.

Even if the program does save money overall, it still poses a political problem: The agencies that save money on health care, for example, are not the same as those that spend money on housing and other services. That could lead to a budget turf war.

Shelters Push Back

The program could also force changes in the shelter community. [Former Massachusetts governor Mitt] Romney appointee Linda Barton Fosburg, executive director of the Massachusetts Interagency Council on Homelessness and Housing, says that some advocates "don't want to see the shelter industry dismantled" because "they don't want to let go of their piece of the pie." Robert V. Hess, commissioner of New York City's Department of Homeless Services, said he has seen "a fair amount of push-back" from shelter providers to the idea of housing first in New York, as well as in Philadelphia, where he introduced it.

But housing-first advocates say that some shelters can adjust programmatically and financially by becoming providers of transitional and permanent housing. Several homeless shelters in the area, such as Father Bill's Place in Quincy, have already started converting.

Yet even as the Massachusetts pilot has shown promise, critics have begun to express other concerns. One, they say, is that success would distract attention from the 80 to 90 percent of the homeless population who are not chronically homeless. Another is that lawmakers will be too quick to reduce funding for the state's many homeless shelters—or that they will try to do housing first on the cheap, which will cause it to fail.

"We don't want to rob Peter to pay Paul," said Lyndia Downie, president of the Pine Street Inn. The state is in dire need, she said, of a comprehensive plan to address homelessness.

Last October, the legislature created a commission to be co-chaired by Rep. Byron Rushing and Tina Brooks, Governor Deval Patrick's undersecretary for Department of Housing and Community Development, to do just that. But Patrick, who has said he is committed to ending homelessness in Massachusetts, has not yet appointed any members.

Harm-Reduction Model

Another open question is how much housing first helps the homeless with their underlying problems. But advocates say that this is a very high bar; addiction, for example, is a notoriously difficult problem, and even modest goals make the idea worthwhile.

"If you measure success as complete abstinence, success rates are very low," said Culhane. "Many people relapse." But "in the public health field, there is a countervailing view, sometimes characterized as harm-reduction." In this view, minimizing harm—as in the case of clean-needles programs to reduce the spread of HIV—is every bit as important.

Joe and Judy, the couple who recently moved into the Dorchester two-bedroom, met five years ago at the Long Island Shelter in Quincy Bay while handing out blankets. On the street for years, they had both spent their nights bouncing from Boston Common park benches to various shelters and back to hang out on the Common during daylight hours. Now HIV positive from sharing needles, Joe says the simple act of taking his lifesaving medications was often thwarted when his small bag of possessions was stolen as he tried to sleep on the streets.

For now, the two appear to be functioning well: They say they have been attending Narcotics Anonymous meetings three times a week, keep the place neat, and cook for themselves. Both say they are clean and want to kick cigarettes next. They say disabilities have kept them from working, but Judy wants to find a job.

"I have a lot more hope," she said.

> "The court gives defendants specially de-
> signed treatment plans that include
> case managers to help get them into
> psychiatric rehabilitation and support-
> ive housing programs, obtain proper
> medications and find assistance to over-
> come drug and alcohol abuse."

Specialized Justice Systems Connect Homeless People with Services

Heather Knight

As San Francisco Chronicle *staff writer Heather Knight reports in the following viewpoint, San Francisco is one of many cities nationwide that is turning to behavioral health courts and enforcement of quality-of-life crimes (such as urinating in public or possession of open alcohol containers) to compel homeless people to participate in and accept much-needed services. Such "problem-solving" courts typically dismiss a defendant's charges after completion of the court program, which usually includes social services and substance abuse or mental health interventions. Such courts, writes Knight, are a bright spot in the crimi-*

nal justice system because they allow homeless people to receive individualized attention and encouragement toward a positive outcome in their lives, perhaps for the first time.

As you read, consider the following questions:

1. What did a study find to be true about participants in San Francisco's Behavioral Health Court?

2. Who can refer a defendant to the Behavioral Health Court?

3. After what is San Francisco's new Community Justice Center modeled?

As debate rages over how to solve San Francisco's seemingly intractable homeless problem, city leaders, academic researchers and even some formerly homeless people themselves say progress is being made every Thursday afternoon inside Department 15 at the city's gloomy Hall of Justice.

For a couple of hours each week, the courtroom fills with dozens of defendants with serious mental illnesses who have been charged with or convicted of crimes ranging from misdemeanor theft to felony assault and robbery. Almost all were homeless or on the brink of living on the streets at the time of their arrests, and many of them struggle with drug or alcohol abuse.

It sounds like a scary scene, like many city residents' worst fears gathered together in one room. But it's surprisingly touching—and according to Superior Court Judge Mary Morgan, who presides over the court, it's "the most hopeful thing happening in the criminal justice system."

On one Thursday not long ago [in late 2007], a bipolar man arrested in March for battery against a BART [Bay Area Rapid Transit] agent brought his trumpet to court on Morgan's orders and stunned the packed courtroom into silence with his rendition of "Somewhere Over the Rainbow."

It's not unusual for defendants to approach the bench to present Morgan with a poem, greeting card or artwork they have crafted just for her or to show her the most recent photograph of their children.

Working with a host of city agencies, the court gives the defendants specially designed treatment plans that include case managers to help them get into psychiatric rehabilitation and supportive housing programs, obtain proper medications and find assistance to overcome drug and alcohol abuse. If the defendants successfully complete the program, which usually takes a year or two, their criminal charges often are reduced or wiped from their record.

But maybe more importantly for the defendants, Morgan and others say, these Thursday sessions could be the first time in a long time anybody's paid attention to them—other than spotting them on the streets and quickly scurrying away.

"We have a lot of cases in here. We're busy making sure they're in compliance with their treatment plan and doing well," said Jennifer Johnson, a lawyer with the public defender's office who represents many of the defendants at the court. "It's nice sometimes to stop and listen to what they're interested in—what moves them."

Lisa Lightman, who directs this and other special courts within the San Francisco Superior Court, said defendants often say the best thing about the court is simply getting noticed.

"That moment makes all the difference for them staying in the program," she said. "Sometimes it's the first time they've been heard by an authority figure—they feel recognized."

Recidivism Curtailed

Behavioral Health Court works, according to a UC [University of California] San Francisco study published in September in the *American Journal of Psychiatry*. The study found that participants in the program, marking its fifth anniversary this month [November 2007], are far less likely to commit future crimes than mentally ill criminals processed through the traditional justice system.

Data indicate that by 18 months after completion, participants, who at first are required to make weekly court appearances, are 39 percent less likely to be charged with a new offense than mentally ill people in the regular court system. The risk of being charged with a new violent crime was 54 percent lower, the study found.

"The participation appears to enhance public safety—not compromise it," said Dale McNeil, one of the authors of the study.

But not everyone is convinced the court is an answer to San Francisco's homelessness problem.

Jennifer Friedenbach, director of the Coalition on Homelessness, said it's one more example of the city offering services to homeless people and the mentally ill only after they become part of the criminal justice system. She and other advocates wonder why these well-regarded services aren't as readily available to mentally ill homeless people outside the courts.

"We just don't have enough treatment for everyone who needs it," she said.

One person who has benefited from the Behavioral Health Court is Maurice Chambers Wilson. On one recent Thursday, the 37-year-old approached the bench and told Morgan about his new room in a single-room-occupancy [SRO] hotel.

"I have the key right here to open the door to my happiness," he told her, waving the little gold-colored key as proof.

"I want you to stay on track and remember how important having a place to live is," Morgan told him before, as she often does, ordering a round of applause for Wilson from the entire courtroom—the burly bailiffs included. (The bailiffs are specially trained to put up with more yelling and other behavior than would be tolerated in traditional courts.)

A Challenging Clientele

Wilson was a homeless alcoholic struggling with manic depression, schizophrenia and bipolar disorder when he said he heard voices one night telling him to hurt someone. He hit a stranger walking across Market Street in the Castro [the Castro District] and was arrested for felony assault.

He spent several months in jail before being selected for the Behavioral Health Court. . . .

When he's not in court on Thursdays, he's likely to pass his days in a dingy building on Market near Fifth Street, which houses Citywide Case Management Forensic Program, the unwieldy name given to the social services component of the court, which is run by UC San Francisco.

There, those participating in the court meet with social workers, join support groups, take classes in art and cooking, play board games and just hang out. If the threat of jail is the stick, this building, which Wilson calls a sanctuary, is the carrot that keeps him and others determined to make it.

"The model of connecting the services to the court does work," said Kathleen Connolly Lacey, program director of Citywide. "There has to be a benefit to people to participate. They work harder than they would if they got straight probation."

She added that the center gives some structure to people who often don't have jobs, aren't in school and aren't raising families.

"They're so highly structured in jail and when they get out, they have nothing to do and that leads to, um, interesting activities," she said.

Wilson's days now consist of working a part-time job running errands for the owner of an art gallery.

"I've made a real turnaround," he said. "I want to be a more productive citizen in society."

The court handles more than 200 cases a year like Wilson's. Many city agencies collaborate with the Superior Court to make it work, including the district attorney and public defender's offices, the departments of Public Health and Adult Probation, the sheriff's department and Jail Psychiatric Services.

Judges, attorneys or staff with Jail Psychiatric Services can refer a defendant to the mental health court, though participation is voluntary. Those who qualify are in jail and have serious mental health problems, such as schizophrenia or bipolar disorder, which directly contributed to the person committing the crime in the first place. Defendants charged with sex offenses, homicide, domestic violence or weapons offenses aren't eligible.

"These are people who are ill and who need treatment for their sake, for the sake of their families, for society at large," Morgan said.

The Goal Is Graduation

Once they become part of the court, the defendants are never homeless. They stay in jail until they can be provided housing, often in SRO hotels in the Tenderloin [a neighborhood in downtown San Francisco].

As they progress through the program, they are required to go to Morgan's Thursday court session less and less often until they "graduate." . . .

The Thursday sessions usually last a couple of hours and consist of each defendant coming to the podium with a public defender or private lawyer to speak with Morgan for a minute or two about their progress.

"Hello, your honor," one man said on a recent Thursday. "I'm a clean and sober person for three months and four days now. And my place is so clean. I go on cleaning spurts!"

"I learned how to make sushi," another told her.

Another showed off his brand-new jacket.

Morgan remains patient and calm with each one, giving many of them a little piece of advice or a compliment.

"You're doing well, so well. . . . Just be patient, OK? Don't give up. . . . Your hair's different! You look great. . . . I hear you have a job at Safeway. . . . You look much better in those clothes than you do in orange. . . . Eat fruits and vegetables—they're the best thing for you. . . . You're the most important person in the world to you, got that?"

But she's also firm when defendants aren't doing well, telling them they risk being booted from the program and returned to the traditional court system if they don't shape up. Often, that means heading straight to state prison.

"You're out of control," she told one recently. "You're doing too much in the way of drinking and doing too much in the way of drugs. You've got one week to get it together."

One who has gotten it together is Sherry Erlandson. The 28-year-old high school dropout struggled with bipolar disorder and a drug addiction and was arrested in late 2004 for felony assault after slamming her then-girlfriend's finger in a door. She used to cry to Morgan every Thursday afternoon.

Now, she lives on her own, takes her medications, speaks about mental illness to the sheriff's department and community groups, started a pet therapy group for the other defendants and holds a job serving food at the social service center's Jitterbug Cafe. She's due to graduate soon.

"I've never graduated from anything—I'm so close now," she said, a huge smile spreading across her face. "I would recommend it to anybody—it's changed my life tremendously. This is my first job ever in my whole entire life—I'm just so happy."

Special Courts Aim for Rehabilitation

The Behavioral Health Court is just one of several "problem-solving courts" within the San Francisco Superior Court.

The model, which is catching on around the nation and in several other countries, aims to go beyond punishing defendants for their crimes by focusing instead on rehabilitation of problems that contributed to the crimes being committed in the first place.

While the Behavioral Health Court focuses on healing defendants' mental illnesses, San Francisco's 12-year-old drug court aims to rein in their drug addictions. Youth with mental illness or substance abuse problems can access services through the Youth Treatment and Education Center, also part of the Superior Court, which includes a special high school for juveniles on probation.

A new problem-solving court—and pet project of Mayor Gavin Newsom—is due to open in April [2008] and tackle misdemeanors and nonviolent felonies including car break-ins and shoplifting that plague the Tenderloin and South of Market neighborhoods.

Called the Community Justice Center, it is modeled on Manhattan's Midtown Community Court. A Superior Court judge will preside over the new court, handing down sentences mixing community service and social services.

Originally, Newsom wanted the court to concentrate on smaller quality-of-life crimes such as public urination and public drunkenness.

But the Superior Court decided to use the court to focus on somewhat more serious crimes, in part because under state law, people issued infractions for quality-of-life crimes cannot be taken into custody and brought straight to court, which is what happens in the New York model. In California, they are issued citations and told to come to traffic court within 45 days.

Supervisor Bevan Dufty, one of City Hall's biggest champions of problem-solving courts, has asked the city controller to prepare a report on how the various courts are working and how the new Community Justice Center will fit in with them. Dufty said he is a huge fan of the Behavioral Health Court and has referred many people from his district to it.

"My experience referring individuals to the Behavioral Health Court has been extremely positive, both for individuals and the neighborhood," Dufty said. "It's a holistic approach that recognizes that much of the state's mental health system has been dismantled over the past generation."

> *"Homeless clients want housing. There currently is not enough of it to go around. Arresting them instead of citing them for sleeping and other basic life activities will not change the availability of the most needed services."*

Enforcing Quality-of-Life Crimes Further Victimizes Homeless People

Amanda Witherell

Homeless people in San Francisco regularly receive criminal citations for doing certain things such as sleeping or urinating in public simply because they do not have a private space in which to do them. The city's logic is that when the homeless report to court for such "quality of life" violations, they can be introduced to helpful social services. But as San Francisco Bay Guardian *investigative reporter Amanda Witherell explains in the following viewpoint, the consequences of handing out such tickets are far from benign. Instead of helping the homeless, according to Witherell, the practice often simply leads instead to an accumulation of misdemeanors, failures to appear, warrants, and then subsequent ineligibility for housing assistance and other services because of having a criminal record. Witherell's critique of the city's quality-of-life enforcement maintains that it is both selectively applied and badly misguided.*

As you read, consider the following questions:

1. What are some of the things the author describes as "status crimes"?

2. According to San Francisco Police Lt. David Lazar, who leads SFPD's homeless outreach team, what are three reasons that homeless people don't want to receive services?

3. What do two homeless advocacy groups have on file with the San Francisco Superior Court?

Sleeping in the park, urinating in public, blocking the sidewalk, trespassing, drinking in public—these and about 10 other infractions are commonly and collectively known as "quality of life" crimes because they affect the condition of the common spaces we all share in San Francisco.

For a homeless individual, they're also called "status" crimes, committed in the commons because there is no private place to sleep, go to the bathroom, or crack a beer. For years the district attorney's [DA's] office hasn't bothered to allocate time or resources to prosecute these petty crimes, and advocates for the rights of homeless people have contended that to do so results in unfair persecution of those who have no place to call home.

Elisa Della-Piana is an attorney with the Lawyers' Committee for Civil Rights [of the San Francisco Bay Area] and has spent much of the past three years in traffic court arguing against fines for homeless people who have received quality-of-life citations. As of this summer [2007], Della-Piana said things have changed down at the Hall of Justice.

Now every time she stands up to represent a homeless person in traffic court, someone from the DA's office gets up too, fighting for the other side. Though there's no way to tell from the traffic court calendar if the defendant is homeless, Della-Piana and Christina Brown, another attorney who represents through the Lawyers' Committee, have witnessed prosecutors ignore quality-of-life citations that didn't appear to have been collected by homeless people.

"When the person is homeless and the DA stands up and prosecutes, that's selective prosecution. They've done that in the past with other populations in San Francisco," Jenny Friedenbach of the Coalition on Homelessness said, citing historic crackdowns on queers and Asians.

Selective Prosecution?

Deputy district attorney Paul Henderson denied the DA's office is selectively prosecuting only quality-of-life citations received by homeless individuals. "We're prosecuting all of them," he told the *Guardian*, confirming this is a new task for the office. "In the past the DA's office wasn't staffed to have people in the courtroom. I think we're there every day now." He said more staff has been hired, and a team he heads is now devoted to the issue.

When asked why this was a new priority for the DA's office, Henderson said, "We felt that people weren't getting the help they needed. The public's interest wasn't being served. [These issues] were not getting addressed in the traffic court without the DA being there. Neighborhoods and communities have been complaining about the lack of responsiveness, and so we're trying to address that."

Henderson called the day in court an open door for a homeless person to walk through and access services. "We want to handle them responsibly to make sure there's some accountability for breaking the law, but try to do it in a way that's an intervention."

But advocates for homeless rights say that's not what happens.

"They'll tell you we're there to offer services to homeless individuals," Della-Piana said. "Which is a piece of paper. In fact, what they have is the same list of services the police pass out. They're not actually doing anything to connect people to the services. They're just offering the list. They could offer those services in the street. There's no reason to go through the court system."

This list of homeless resources is updated every six months by the San Francisco Police Department's Operation Outreach and is offered on the street, according to Lt. David Lazar, leader of the 20-officer branch of the SFPD [San Francisco Police Department] that interfaces directly with the homeless population.

Barriers to Service

"The accountability is a problem, and the process they go through is not working," Lazar said. "There's a large population we're seeing that doesn't want services." He listed three reasons: inadequacies in the shelter system, a desire to be left alone, and a mental health or substance abuse problem that impairs judgment. "If we could house absolutely everyone, what would they do during the daytime?" he asked. "You need intensive case management, job support, substance abuse support."

But homeless-rights advocates say the stability of housing is the first step toward improving the quality of life for the homeless. Della-Piana said, "Ninety-five percent of my clients come to me and say, 'I'm getting social services.' They point to something on the list and say, 'I'm doing this.' They're doing everything they're supposed to be doing, but they don't have housing yet. That's why people are still sleeping in the park."

Henderson said critics of the new tack "aren't recognizing that laws are being broken. People's qualities of life are being

Types of Homeless Criminalization Measures

The criminalization of homelessness takes many forms, including:

- Enactment and enforcement of legislation that makes it illegal to sleep, sit, or store personal belongings in public spaces in cities where people are forced to live in public spaces.

- Selective enforcement of more neutral laws, such as loitering, jaywalking, or open container laws, against homeless persons.

- Sweeps of city areas in which homeless persons are living to drive them out of those areas, frequently resulting in the destruction of individuals' personal property such as important personal documents and medication.

- Enactment and enforcement of laws that punish people for begging or panhandling in order to move poor or homeless persons out of a city or downtown area.

- Enactment and enforcement of laws that restrict groups sharing food with homeless persons in public spaces.

- Enforcement of a wide range of so-called "quality of life" ordinances related to public activities and hygiene (i.e., public urination) when no public facilities are available to people without housing.

National Law Center on Homelessness & Poverty
and National Coalition for the Homeless,
Homes Not Handcuffs: The Criminalization of
Homelessness in U.S. Cities. *Washington, DC:*
NLCHP/NCH, 2009.

dragged down by these violations. If it's your street, your door, and there's feces on it every day, that affects your quality of life."

Ticketing the homeless is not a new thing. Two homeless-rights groups—Religious Witness with Homeless People and the Coalition on Homelessness—have a standing Freedom of Information Act request with San Francisco Superior Court that provides a monthly tally of the infractions likely committed primarily by homeless people. According to their data, for the past 15 years the SFPD has averaged about 13,000 quality-of-life citations per year. Last year Religious Witness released a study showing that more than 31,000 citations had been issued during Mayor Gavin Newsom's administration.

Citations Have Big Price Tags

"For the police, the sheriff, and the court cost, we estimated it cost almost $6 million for those 31,000 citations," said Sister Bernie Galvin, executive director of Religious Witness. Galvin said a new study, to be released at City Hall on Oct. 4, shows that citations and costs have skyrocketed in the past 14 months. "Now we're putting in the dramatic new expense of the DA," she said, adding, "Everyone wants to prosecute a greater number. It's like it makes it justifiable to issue these 31,000 tickets if we can prosecute them. Actually, it makes it crueler and more expensive."

Media reports have characterized the tickets as empty pieces of paper, issued and then metaphorically shredded when a homeless individual fails to pay the $50 to $500 fine. In a recent *San Francisco Chronicle* story, Heather Knight reported that "all quality-of-life citations are getting dismissed." Yet when they don't—and violators either don't show up in court or can't pay the fine—infractions become misdemeanors or an arrest warrant is issued, both of which become problems for people trying to access services.

"It backfires," said Christina Brown, an associate at O'Melveny and Myers who volunteers time in traffic court representing homeless people through the Lawyers' Committee. "When people are served with warrants, they're precluded from services." Even if the person cuts a deal with the DA to access services in lieu of paying a fine, they still have to return to court to prove they've done that. If they can't get the paperwork or can't make it to the court in time, it becomes a misdemeanor.

"The criminal justice system is actually making it harder if they want to find somewhere else to sleep," said Della-Piana, who related an anecdote of a client who had a few open-container infractions. The client was afraid to go to court when she couldn't pay the fines, so a warrant was issued. She'd spent the past seven years on the Department of Housing and Urban Development's waiting list for public housing and got kicked off because of the misdemeanor.

Legislating Services

Public Defender Jeff Adachi expressed concern that a dragnet is being created for arresting homeless people committing status crimes they have no control over. "We have to be very careful we're not trying to legislate services through the criminal justice system. We do too much of that already," he said. "This approach assumes that if a person is in trouble, they're more likely to accept the services. I haven't seen that is true."

Henderson doesn't necessarily agree that the criminal justice system shouldn't play a role in assisting homeless people: "I want this citation to serve as a wake-up call for you." He thinks people need to be held accountable and would like to see the city adopt the plan for a Community Justice Center, modeled after New York City's, a vision that his boss, District Attorney Kamala Harris, and Newsom also share.

"We believe San Francisco has a unique infrastructure and need for the Community Justice Center. That's why we are proposing to pilot this initiative in the Tenderloin and South of Market area, where more than a third of the city's quality-of-life offenses occur," Harris and Newsom wrote in a May 13 editorial in the *Chronicle*. "The center promises to give relief to the neighborhoods most affected by quality-of-life crimes."

During an Oct. 1 endorsement interview with the *Guardian*, Newsom said he hoped to open the new center by December. Lazar, who sits on the committee that's still hammering out the details for how exactly the center would work, agreed with Henderson that it's the next step in more direct connection with services: "We're trying to put the criminal justice system and the social justice system together."

Della-Piana said this still ignores the black marks that misdemeanors leave, which become good reasons for some service providers to save their limited resources for people with clean records. "The two ideologies don't mesh," Della-Piana said. "My homeless clients want housing. There currently is not enough of it to go around. Arresting them instead of citing them for sleeping and other basic life activities will not change the availability of the most needed services."

Periodical and Internet Sources Bibliography

The following articles have been selected to supplement the diverse views presented in this chapter.

Paul Boden	"It's Crazy to Criminalize Homelessness," *Huffington Post*, January 20, 2011. www.huffingtonpost.com.
Martha R. Burt	"Life After Transitional Housing for Homeless Families," Urban Institute, March 2010. www.urban.org.
Barbara Ehrenreich	"Is It Now a Crime to Be Poor?," *New York Times*, August 8, 2009. www.nytimes.com.
Javier C. Hernandez	"Despite the Mayor's Homeless Program, Many Return to Shelters, Critics Say," *New York Times*, December 8, 2010. www.nytimes.com.
George L. Kelling	"How New York Became Safe: The Full Story," *City Journal*, July 17, 2009. www.city-journal.org.
Douglas L. Polcin	"A Model for Sober Housing During Outpatient Treatment," *Journal of Psychoactive Drugs*, vol. 41, no. 2, June 2009.
Jim Salter	"FEMA Weighs Housing Options for Homeless Tornado Victims," Associated Press, May 31, 2011.
Sam Skolnik	"Growing Homeless Settlement Vexes Business, Goodman," *Las Vegas Sun*, April 3, 2009. www.lasvegassun.com.
Michael Winerip	"Homeless, but Finding Sanctuary at School," *New York Times*, May 1, 2011. www.nytimes.com.

CHAPTER 4

What Policies Will Reduce Homelessness?

Chapter Preface

Sometimes it can seem that there are as many approaches to reducing homelessness as there are social service organizations, charities, and government agencies to provide them. As the authors in the following chapter discuss, housing vouchers, emergency shelters, housing-first programs, street-team interventions, governmental ten-year plans, donation meters, street newspapers, and outreach projects targeting the chronically homeless all typically enjoy bipartisan support, and each plays a role in reducing the number of people who experience homelessness on any given night in this country. Other efforts to reduce homelessness, however, are more controversial. One such approach is the increasingly popular practice of giving homeless individuals a free, one-way bus or plane ticket out of town to wherever they have family. In San Francisco, for example, from 2004 to 2009 more than four thousand homeless people were sent to other cities through the city's Homeward Bound Program, according to the Mayor's Office. Las Vegas, Nevada; New York, New York; Atlantic City, New Jersey; St. Petersburg, Florida; Colorado Springs, Colorado; and Lancaster, California, are among the other cities nationwide that have similar homeless repatriation programs.

Economics is the main driving force of the movement because the homeless create a big drain on a city's budget; they utilize public services such as police, fire, and medical at very high rates, and operating shelters and offering services to them is quite costly. As the *New York Times* reported in 2009, New York City paid for more than 550 families to leave the city over two years; the move saved the city millions because it kept those families from entering the city's expensive shelter system, which costs $36,000 a year per family.

Proponents of the practice maintain that besides saving money, it reunites estranged family members and puts vulnerable individuals where they are most likely to succeed—that is, close to their natural support systems of kith and kin. Meanwhile, critics argue that a big difference exists between reducing homelessness and simply reducing the appearance of homelessness. According to Arnold Cohen, president of Partnership for the Homeless, an advocacy group in New York, busing homeless people out of town is nothing more than a shell game. "The city is engaged in cosmetics," Cohen told the *New York Times* in a 2009 interview. "What we're doing is passing the problem of homelessness to another city. We're taking people from a shelter bed here to the living room couch of another family. Essentially, this family is still homeless."

Homeless experts agree that if people are living on the street, the likelihood that they have strong familial support systems elsewhere is not very good, and it is difficult for homeless individuals to start a new life simply by moving to another city. Not surprisingly, neighboring cities and counties often end up providing homeless services to relocated individuals once they arrive in their area and things don't work out the way they envisioned. Some cities have leveled charges of "homeless dumping" at larger municipalities that direct a large number of homeless people to their area, such as is the case with Lancaster, California, and its larger neighbor, Los Angeles. Similarly, after complaints from neighboring Humboldt County, San Francisco agreed to give Humboldt notice when its homeless take the city up on its offer for a free ticket to that county.

Whether sending homeless people back to their cities of origin actually helps people put life on the streets behind them—or whether it simply moves the problem to another location—remains to be seen, but the initiative is another in the long line of ideas put forth with the goal of reducing homelessness.

> "Researchers and policy makers are newly optimistic about the prospect of ending homelessness."

Better Information About Homelessness Means Better Strategies

Dennis Culhane

In the following viewpoint, University of Pennsylvania professor of social policy Dennis Culhane debunks several myths about homelessness and explains that a better understanding of homeless individuals and their circumstances opens the way for innovative approaches to solving what was once considered an intractable societal problem. Culhane looks at common assumptions about mental illness, unemployment, homeless shelters, and other issues, and he systematically refutes those assumptions with research. He also points out that many previous public policies on homelessness were based on faulty assumptions and actually made the problem worse. Culhane is also the director of research for the National Center on Homelessness Among Veterans.

As you read, consider the following questions:

1. According to the author, why do people falsely conclude that the deinstitutionalization of psychiatric patients contributed to the increase in homelessness?

2. What did a national study by the Urban Institute reveal about the work habits of homeless people?

3. How does the author say that the function of homeless shelters changed as they grew and became more entrenched over the years?

Last month [in June 2010], the [Barack] Obama administration released a plan designed to end homelessness in 10 years. The goal reflects new optimism among academics and advocates that homelessness is not an intractable feature of urban life, as it has sometimes seemed, but a problem that can be solved. This belief is fueled by recent research debunking a number of long-standing myths about homelessness in America—and showing that many of our old policies were unwittingly making the problem worse.

1. Homelessness is usually a long-term condition. To the contrary, the most common length of time that someone is homeless is one or two days, and half the people who enter the homeless shelter system will leave within 30 days, never to return.

Long-term homelessness is relatively rare. According to the Department of Housing and Urban Development [HUD], about 2 million people in the United States were homeless at some point in 2009 (meaning they stayed overnight in a shelter or in a place not meant for human habitation). But on any given day, only about 112,000 people fit the federal definition of "chronic homelessness," which applies to those who have been continuously homeless for a year or more, or are experiencing at least their fourth episode of homelessness in three years.

Nearly all of the long-term homeless have tenuous family ties and some kind of disability, whether it is a drug or alcohol addiction, a mental illness, or a physical handicap. While they make up a small share of the homeless population, they are disproportionately costly to society: They consume nearly 60 percent of the resources spent on emergency and transitional shelter for adults, and they occupy hospitals and jails at high rates.

Damaging Misconceptions

2. Most of the homeless have a severe mental illness. Because the relatively small number of people living on the streets who suffer from paranoia, delusions and other mental disorders are very visible, they have come to stand for the entire homeless population—despite the fact that they are in the minority. As a result, many people falsely concluded that an increase in homelessness in the 1980s resulted from the deinstitutionalization of psychiatric care in the 1960s and 1970s.

In my own research, I have calculated that the rate of severe mental illness among the homeless (including families and children) is 13 to 15 percent. Among the much smaller group of single adults who are chronically homeless, however, the rate reaches 30 to 40 percent. For this population, mental illness is clearly a barrier to exiting homelessness.

But depending on a community's resources, having a severe mental illness may, paradoxically, protect against homelessness. Poor people with severe psychiatric disabilities may have more means of support than other people in poverty because they are eligible for a modest federal disability income, Medicaid, and housing and support services designed specifically for them. Not so for the other childless singles—including ex-convicts, people with drug addictions and the able-bodied unemployed—who make up the majority of the nation's homeless population.

3. Homeless people don't work. According to a 2002 national study by the Urban Institute, about 45 percent of homeless adults had worked in the past 30 days—only 14 percentage points lower than the employment rate for the general population last month. The number of working homeless would probably be even higher if "off the books" work was included. Whether scavenging for scrap metal or staffing shelters, many homeless people adopt ingenious ways to subsist.

A recent job loss is the second most common reason people say they became homeless. In a study my colleagues and I are completing, we observe a steep drop in earned income in the year prior to the onset of homelessness. Interestingly, those people who return to work show a steep recovery in earned income three years after their initial homeless spell. Our preliminary data also suggest that about a third of the chronically homeless eventually end up working, thanks, quite likely, to substance-abuse recovery.

4. Shelters are a humane solution to homelessness. When homelessness became a national epidemic in the 1980s, reformers responded with emergency shelters that were meant to be temporary havens. But as homelessness became more entrenched, so did shelters: Their capacity more than doubled by the late 1980s, then again a few years later, and then again by 2000. Along the way, they became institutionalized way stations for lots of poor people with temporary housing crises, including those avoiding family conflicts, leaving prison or transitioning from substance-abuse treatment.

Large shelters are notoriously overcrowded and often unruly places where people experience the ritualized indignities of destitution: long lines for bedding or a squeeze of toothpaste; public showers; thieves; conflict. Many people have voted with their feet, and as a result, street homelessness persists.

Solutions to End Homelessness for Good

Shelters may be the final safety net, but that net scrapes perilously close to the ground. To be in a shelter is to be homeless, and the more shelters we build, the more resources we divert from the only real solution to homelessness: permanent housing.

5. *These poor you will always have with you.* Researchers and policy makers are newly optimistic about the prospect of ending homelessness. For two decades, the goal of our homeless programs was to first treat people for their myriad afflictions (substance abuse, say, or illness) and hope that this would lead them out of homelessness. Now, the attention has shifted to the endgame: Get people back into housing as quickly as possible, the new thinking goes, and the treatment for everything else can quickly follow—and with greater benefits.

People who haven't had a private residence in years have succeeded in these new "housing first" programs, which place the homeless directly into their own housing units, bypassing shelters. Rent is subsidized and services are provided to help these tenants maintain their housing and be good neighbors.

According to HUD, the government has funded more than 70,000 such housing units since 2001. Meanwhile, the number of chronically homeless nationwide has decreased by a third since 2005, to 112,000.

The Obama administration's new Homelessness Prevention and Rapid Re-Housing Program takes a similar approach, giving people suffering temporary housing crises modest cash and service support, allowing them to avoid shelters or get out of them more quickly.

The cost of these programs is partly offset by reductions in expensive hospitalizations, arrests and shelter stays by the chronically homeless—to say nothing of the moral victory a society can claim in caring for its most vulnerable.

"The federal government needs to be smarter and more targeted in its response and role, which also includes supporting the work that is being done on the ground."

Government Initiatives Can Reduce Homelessness

US Interagency Council on Homelessness

The following viewpoint comes from the United States Interagency Council on Homelessness (USICH), which was established by the landmark Stewart B. McKinney Homeless Assistance Act of 1987. The USICH acts independently within the government's executive branch to review the effectiveness of federal homeless assistance activities and policies, promote coordination among programs, and inform state and local governments and public and private organizations about the availability of federal programs serving the homeless. This viewpoint reflects the council's work on the first ever Federal Strategic Plan to Prevent and End Homelessness, *which it presented to President Barack*

Obama in 2010. The plan establishes an ambitious time line for eliminating specific types of homelessness and sets forth a comprehensive strategy for ultimately ending all homelessness in America.

As you read, consider the following questions:

1. According to the authors, what effect will the Obama administration's health care reform have on the *Federal Strategic Plan to Prevent and End Homelessness*?

2. What does the plan promise will be achieved by increasing collaboration at all levels of government?

3. The authors say that the nineteen agencies that make up the USICH are making a strong commitment to prevent and end homelessness by doing what?

Our nation has made significant progress over the last decade [2000–2010] reducing homelessness in specific communities and with specific populations. Communities across the United States—from rural Mankato, Minnesota, to urban San Francisco—have organized partnerships between local and state agencies and with the private and nonprofit sectors to implement plans to prevent, reduce, and end homelessness. These communities, in partnership with the federal government, have used a targeted pipeline of resources to combine housing and supportive services to deliver permanent supportive housing for people who have been homeless the longest and are the frailest. The results have been significant.

In many respects, this current period of economic hardship mirrors the early 1980s when widespread homelessness reappeared for the first time since the Great Depression. Communities will need all of the tools in our grasp to meet the needs of those experiencing homelessness, including families and far too many of our nation's veterans. In particular, we are concerned that recent national data show a significant rise in family homelessness from 2008 to 2009.

HUD [the US Department of Housing and Urban Development] Secretary Shaun Donovan, HHS [Department of Health and Human Services] Secretary Kathleen Sebelius, VA [Department of Veterans Affairs] Secretary Eric K. Shinseki, and Labor Secretary Hilda Solis declared the vision of the Plan to be centered on the belief that "no one should experience homelessness—no one should be without a safe, stable place to call home." The Plan is focused on four key goals:

1. Finish the job of ending chronic homelessness in five years;

2. Prevent and end homelessness among veterans in five years;

3. Prevent and end homelessness for families, youth, and children in ten years; and

4. Set a path to ending all types of homelessness.

The goals and time frames we aspire to in this Plan are an important target for the nation. They demonstrate the council's belief that ending homelessness in America must be a priority for our country. As President Barack Obama has said, in a nation as wealthy as ours, "it is simply unacceptable for individuals, children, families, and our nation's veterans to be faced with homelessness." We believe it is important to set goals, even if aspirational, for true progress to be made.

A National Road Map

This Plan is a road map for joint action by the 19-member United States Interagency Council on Homelessness [USICH] along with local and state partners in the public and private sectors. It will provide a reference framework for the allocation of resources and the alignment of programs to achieve our goal to prevent and end homelessness in America. The Plan also proposes the realignment of existing programs based on what we have learned and the best practices that are occurring at the local level, so that resources focus on what works. We will take action in partnership with Congress, states, localities, philanthropy, and communities around the country.

From years of practice and research, we have identified successful approaches to end homelessness. Evidence points to the role housing plays as an essential platform for human and community development. Stable housing is the foundation upon which people build their lives—absent a safe, decent, affordable place to live, it is next to impossible to achieve good health, positive educational outcomes, or reach one's economic potential. Indeed, for many persons living in poverty, the lack of stable housing leads to costly cycling through crisis-driven systems like foster care, emergency rooms, psychiatric hospitals, emergency domestic violence shelters, detox centers, and jails. By the same token, stable housing provides an ideal launching pad for the delivery of health care and other social services focused on improving life outcomes for individuals and families. More recently, researchers have focused on housing stability as an important ingredient for the success of children and youth in school. When children have a stable home, they are more likely to succeed socially, emotionally, and academically.

Capitalizing on these insights, this Plan builds on the significant reforms of the last decade and the intent by the Obama administration to directly address homelessness through intergovernmental collaboration. Successful implementation of this Plan will result in stability and permanency for the more than 640,000 men, women, and children who are homeless on a single day in America. At the same time, its execution will produce approaches to homelessness that are cost-effective for local, state, and federal government. The Plan's content presents initial goals, themes, objectives, and strategies and was generated through the collaboration and consensus of the 19 USICH member agencies. Since the Homeless Emergency Assistance and Rapid Transition to

Housing (HEARTH) Act requires USICH to update the Plan annually, the substance of this Plan represents the beginning of a process toward our goal of preventing and ending homelessness.

The Affordable Care Act

The Affordable Care Act (Health Reform), a landmark initiative of the Obama administration, will further the Plan's goals by helping numerous families and individuals experiencing homelessness to get the health care they need. Medicaid will be expanded to nearly all individuals under the age of 65 with incomes up to 133 percent of the federal poverty level (currently about $15,000 for a single individual). This significant expansion will allow more families and adults without dependent children to enroll in Medicaid in 2014. In addition, Health Reform will support demonstrations to improve the ability of psychiatric facilities to provide emergency services. It will also expand the availability of medical homes for individuals with chronic conditions, including severe and persistent mental illness. Expansion of Community Health Centers is another major change that will serve many vulnerable populations, including those who are homeless or at risk of being homeless.

The Plan proposes a set of strategies that call upon the federal government to work in partnership with state and local governments, as well as the private sector to employ cost effective, comprehensive solutions to end homelessness. The Plan recognizes that the federal government needs to be smarter and more targeted in its response and role, which also includes supporting the work that is being done on the ground. The federal government's partners at the local level have already made tremendous strides, with communities across the nation—including over 1,000 mayors and county executives across the country—having developed plans to end homelessness. The Plan highlights that by collaborating at all

Letter from President Barack Obama

Since the founding of our country, "home" has been the center of the American dream. Stable housing is the foundation upon which everything else in a family's or individual's life is built—without a safe, affordable place to live, it is much tougher to maintain good health, get a good education or reach your full potential.

When I took office in January 2009, too many of our fellow citizens were experiencing homelessness. We took decisive action through the American Recovery and Reinvestment Act by investing $1.5 billion in the new Homelessness Prevention and Rapid Re-Housing Program. We have made record Federal investments in targeted homeless assistance in the FY [fiscal year] 2010 budget and FY2011 budget request. And the recently passed Affordable Care Act will provide new and more effective methods for targeting uninsured, chronically ill individuals as well as children, youth, and adults experiencing homelessness. . . .

But there is still much more work to do. Veterans should never find themselves on the streets, living without care and without hope. . . . The previous Administration [of George W. Bush] began the work to end chronic homelessness. Now is the time to challenge our Nation to aspire to end homelessness across *all* populations—including families, youth, children, and veterans. . . .

Now more than ever, we have a responsibility to tackle national challenges like homelessness in the most cost-effective ways possible. Instead of simply responding once a family or a person becomes homeless, prevention and innovation must be at the forefront of our efforts.

President Barack Obama, "Preface,"
Opening Doors: Federal Strategic Plan
to Prevent and End Homelessness,
US Interagency Council on Homelessness, 2010.

levels of government, the nation can harness public resources and build on the innovations that have been demonstrated at the local level and in cities nationwide to provide everyone—from the most capable to the most vulnerable—the opportunity to reach their full potential.

Objectives and Strategies

The Plan includes 10 objectives and 52 strategies. These objectives and strategies contribute to accomplishing all four goals of the Plan.

The first section details the development of this first-ever comprehensive federal plan to prevent and end homelessness. This section sets out the core values reflected in the Plan and the key principles that guided the process. It also describes the opportunities for public comment offered during the development of the Plan.

The second section of the Plan provides an overview of homelessness in America. Since homelessness takes many different forms by population or geographic area, we provide a synopsis of the issues facing these varying groups experiencing homelessness. The section also addresses the sources of data used throughout the Plan.

The third section represents the core of the Plan including the objectives and strategies to prevent and end homelessness. It provides the logic behind each objective, the departments and agencies involved, the key partners, and strategies to achieve the respective objectives.

The Plan concludes with a section that defines the steps USICH partners will take next, providing a framework for action. This includes the impact we aspire to have that will require active work from many partners at all levels of government and across the private sector. This section provides a brief summary about the context in which we move forward in terms of the economic, policy, and political challenges and opportunities. There is a discussion of the measures that will be used to track progress over time toward the Plan goals. Initiatives currently under way that help advance the Plan goals are summarized. Finally, the section lays out the documents USICH will produce to provide information and transparency to the public, Congress, and our partners going forward. . . .

A Strong Commitment

Over the last 30 years, the number of people experiencing homelessness in America has steadily increased. More children and youth than ever do not have a safe and stable place to call home. As Veterans Affairs Secretary Eric K. Shinseki has said, "Those who have served this nation as veterans should never find themselves on the streets, living without care and without hope." Nearly two million service men and women have served in Afghanistan and Iraq; they deserve the top quality care they were promised and the benefits that they have earned.

Simultaneously, while homelessness has grown, our knowledge about what can be done to prevent and end homelessness has also increased. As the first ever comprehensive *Federal Strategic Plan to Prevent and End Homelessness. Opening Doors* is a road map for what we must all do to change the landscape of homelessness in America.

Each of the 19 USICH member agencies is making a strong commitment to the goal of preventing and ending homelessness by agreeing to these goals and strategies and establishing targets and performance measures. We understand action involving unprecedented collaboration must be taken. No one should experience homelessness—no one should be without a safe, stable place to call home.

> "Private social programs are better than government initiatives in ministering to the whole person, rather than treating those in trouble as numbers and prescribing only a check or bed."

Reducing Homelessness Is Not the Government's Responsibility

Doug Bandow

Government programs are not the right answer for helping homeless individuals or families, argues Doug Bandow, former special assistant to President Ronald Reagan and a senior fellow at the Cato Institute, a conservative think tank. The best responses to homelessness, claims Bandow, are human rather than political. In the following viewpoint, he calls upon homeless individuals themselves to practice moral responsibility for their behavior; he calls upon their families and friends to lend a hand in times of need; and he calls upon churches and other community organizations to provide financial assistance and other aid. Local initiatives such as these, Bandow maintains, are far more effective than state or federal efforts to provide help. Bandow advocates

Doug Bandow, "Handling America's Homeless Families," *The Washington Times*, May 17, 2009. Copyright © 2009 by The Washington Times. All rights reserved. Reproduced by permission.

cutting federal subsidies for housing and instead making housing less expensive by changing restrictive zoning laws and building codes.

As you read, consider the following questions:

1. According to the author, what should be the first line of defense against homelessness?

2. How does the author believe the government safety net is best maintained?

3. What does the author argue has limited the housing supply and increased housing costs?

With the economy in apparent free fall, human needs, including homelessness, have grown. Our starting point should be moral, not political.

During the dramatic biblical parable of the sheep and goats, Jesus asserts our moral responsibility rather than debates our policy approach.

Matthew quotes Jesus as telling the sheep: "For I was hungry and you gave me something to eat, I was thirsty and you gave me something to drink, I was a stranger and you invited me in." They ministered to Jesus by doing these things "for one of the least of these brothers of mine."

This duty cannot be subcontracted to government. The Bible demonstrates concentric rings of responsibility moving outward, starting with individuals who are enjoined to take care of themselves, rather than living off of others. Those who fail to care for their families are worse than unbelievers, Paul warns. The early church transferred money within and among faith communities. Finally, Paul says in Galatians, "let us do good to all people."

If the political authorities are to act, it should be because other institutions have failed to meet people's basic needs. Today, far more private than public programs serve the homeless. The Catholic and Protestant doctrines of subsidiarity and sphere sovereignty, respectively, recognize that government is to respect the roles of other social institutions.

Diversity of responses is particularly important in dealing with a problem as complicated as homelessness. Even the number of homeless is disputed.

The Department of Housing and Urban Development [HUD] figures homelessness on any particular night (in or out of a shelter) ran 672,000 as of January 2007—down about 10 percent from 2005. There were 84,000 homeless households, down 15 percent. Chronic homelessness ran 124,000, down 30 percent.

The drop is positive, though these numbers remain far too high, and may have turned up in the current economic imbroglio.

Addressing the Root Problems

The reasons for homelessness run the gamut. Those in poverty long have had difficulty finding affordable housing.

Dubious mortgages, declining home prices and increasing unemployment are threatening many homeowners today. The rising tide of foreclosures puts entire families at risk.

Homelessness also often reflects personal crisis, such as family breakdown, substance abuse and/or mental illness. The deinstitutionalization movement, which sought to respect the dignity of those who had been forcibly medicated and hospitalized, left some people living on the streets. Alcohol or drug use often accentuated other problems.

The answer is not simply more money for more government programs, of which there are thousands nationwide. This enormous challenge can be best met by reflecting back on the biblical model. We need to simultaneously meet current needs, which often include illness and hunger, and reduce future problems.

First, individuals and families have a moral as well as practical imperative to behave responsibly. Americans need to relearn how to resist substance abuse, curb wasteful expenditures and save money. Borrowers and lenders alike should spend money wisely.

Second, family and friends, backed by churches and other social networks, should be the first line of defense to homelessness. The need may be as simple as temporary financial aid or an empty couch. Such informal assistance can soften the impact of unexpected hardship while preserving the dignity of those in need.

Third, private social programs are better than government initiatives in ministering to the whole person, rather than treating those in trouble as numbers and prescribing only a check or bed. Some of the neediest require proverbial "tough love"—compassion and discipline. It is important to keep people off the street and ensure that they won't face the same problem again. That often requires changes in behavior as well as circumstance.

Obviously, charities have been affected by the current economic slump. However, this provides an opportunity for advocacy by activists and preaching by religious leaders. Those concerned about the needy must remind all of us of our duty to help, especially in difficult times. To whom much is given, much is expected, the Bible explains.

The Safety Net Should Be Local

Fourth, local initiatives are most likely to be effective in meeting needs that vary dramatically by region. Unfortunately, the results of many of the federal welfare programs, including those directed at housing, ranging from rental vouchers to Section 8 to public housing, have been ugly. The government's safety net is best maintained by states and localities rather than by Washington [DC].

Fifth, the many federal subsidy programs used to encourage homeownership—Federal Housing Administration, Community Reinvestment Act, Fannie Mae, Freddie Mac—are ground zero of today's housing crisis and should be curbed. Attempts to solve the current crisis by artificially reinflating home values risk rewarding improvident lenders and borrowers alike, delaying painful but necessary adjustments in the housing market, and creating conditions for repeat experience in the near future.

We should instead make housing less expensive. Through exclusionary zoning (including restrictions on multifamily housing and minimum-lot size and square-footage requirements) and outmoded building codes (which reflect union interests rather than safety concerns), government has limited the housing supply and increased housing costs. Palliatives like rent control only worsen the underlying problem; government should strip away barriers to affordable housing. Doing so would help reduce homelessness.

Good people in a good society take care of those in need. That includes the homeless. But just as the problem is complex, so is the solution. And we will do best if we respond first at a human rather than at a political level.

| "*Most cities using donation meters have tried enforcing anti-panhandling laws without success.*"

Donation Meters Are the Best Way to Give Spare Change to the Homeless

Marisa Kendall

As USA Today *staff writer Marisa Kendall explains in the following viewpoint, to combat aggressive panhandling by homeless people, a growing number of cities nationwide are trying out a new approach—installing parking meters that collect coin donations for homeless services rather than parking fees. While proponents of the meters say they are a good way to cut down on panhandling in business districts and ensure that spare change that's donated is put to good use, homeless-rights advocates say it is just a way to push homeless people further out of sight and out of mind. As Kendall writes here, cities across the country have had varying results from the meters, with collection meters in some areas bringing in substantial money to help the homeless and those in other areas doing rather poorly.*

As you read, consider the following questions:

1. According to the author, what do homeless-rights advocates say is the real purpose of the donation meters?

2. What does National Coalition for the Homeless (NCH) speaker David Pirtle say is the biggest danger of donation meters?

3. What does NCH executive director Neil Donovan suggest doing as an alternative to either donating to a meter or a panhandler?

If you passed a homeless person and a metal donation-collecting machine on your way home, which would get your spare change?

A growing number of cities, including Nashville, Virginia Beach and Las Vegas this year [2010] have begun encouraging the latter by providing revamped parking meters for donations—a move some homeless advocates oppose.

The program has been established in at least 16 cities, according to Neil Donovan, executive director of the National Coalition for the Homeless (NCH). Donations deposited in meters go to local charity organizations to provide services such as housing, meals, counseling and job training to the city's homeless, he says.

Homeless-rights advocates who criticize the program say the meters are just a way to expel panhandlers from city limits.

"The NCH believes that communities whenever possible should preserve the relationship of one individual supporting the other . . . and meters intercept that relationship," Donovan says.

Other cities using donation meters include Atlanta, Baltimore, Cleveland, Dallas, Denver, Little Rock, San Francisco and Seattle, he says.

Virginia Beach installed seven bright red donation meters in August, says Mike Eason, the city's resort administrator. The goal is to educate the public and redirect money to centralized charity organizations, he says.

"Each year, thousands of dollars are given to homeless individuals without truly knowing where the money is going," Eason says.

Kirk Welch, executive director of the Judeo-Christian Outreach Center, a homeless aid organization in Virginia Beach, says he does not think the meters will meet their goal of stopping aggressive panhandling.

David Pirtle, a speaker for NCH, was homeless from 2004 through 2006. He says the biggest danger of the donation meters is that they could reinforce negative stereotypes.

"The worst thing about being homeless is the way people treat you," Pirtle says. "If you walk by a panhandler and just ignore them, that just shatters them." The degree of success the meters experience varies greatly depending on the city.

Denver and Cleveland

Denver installed the meters in 2007 and raises about $100,000 a year through more than 80 of them, says Amber Callender, executive director of Denver's Road Home, a program working to end homelessness in Denver. About $30,000 of this is from coin donations and $70,000 is from the sponsorship of businesses and residents who pay $1,000 a year to sponsor a meter, Callender says. The program uses recycled parking meters placed along established meter collection routes, so no installation or collection fees are taken from the proceeds, she says.

Cleveland installed 12 donation meters in the summer of 2009 and has since doubled that number, says Mark Lammon, special projects manager of the Downtown Cleveland Alliance. The total installation and refurbishing cost was about $3,400. During the first year the meters were in place—June 2009–

Donation Meter Programs Nationwide

Atlanta, Georgia, unveiled a donation meter program in September 2008 that when reevaluated by city officials in March 2009 raised only $500.

Baltimore, Maryland, created meters that, instead of counting down minutes, count down from "Hope" to "Despair." The program raised nearly $5,000 in its first year.

Chattanooga, Tennessee, installed thirteen donation meters as part of the city's "Art of Change" program.

Cleveland, Ohio, placed fifteen lime green and red parking meters in the city to raise money for the Downtown Cleveland Alliance's Downtown Homeless Fund.

Denver, Colorado's "Denver's Road Home" campaign began with thirty-six meters in March 2007; by October 2008 there were eighty-six meters. The initiative is part of Denver's ten-year plan to end homelessness.

Little Rock, Akansas, installed twenty-five orange "Change for the Better" boxes. The funds from the boxes are distributed to five area organizations.

Portland, Oregon's "Real Change, Not Spare Change" meter program has raised nearly $10,000 to date [in 2009].

Tempe, Arizona, installed bright red refurbished meters in March 2008. Funds gathered from the "Change for Change" meters are distributed to four different agencies.

Text adapted from: National Law Center on Homelessness & Poverty and National Coalition for the Homeless, Homes Not Handcuffs: The Criminalization of Homelessness in U.S. Cities. *Washington, DC: NLCHP/NCH, 2009.*

June 2010—the meters made about $100 per week for a total of about $5,200. That number has dropped in recent months to $20 per week, Lammon said.

Tulin Ozdeger, civil rights program director for the National Law Center on Homelessness & Poverty, says most cities using donation meters have tried enforcing anti-panhandling laws without success.

Since installing the meters, Denver has reduced its number of panhandlers on one main street by 80%, Callender says.

"We're pretty proud of that reduction," she says.

Orlando will probably install donation meters by the end of this year if the City Council approves the measure, says City Spokesperson Heather Allebaugh.

A 2009 report by the NCH and the National Law Center ranked Orlando the third "meanest" city in the USA to the homeless. In Orlando, people can panhandle only when inside special blue boxes painted on the sidewalks. The city just reduced the number of blue boxes from 36 to 27 on Sept. 13 Allebaugh says.

The Homeless Perspective

Mark Baca, 51, has been homeless since April 2009 and recently entered a Denver rehabilitation center. He is skeptical about whether he will ever see the money that goes into donation meters.

"The only time I've seen the donations go straight to the homeless people is when a car pulls up, opens up the back and starts pulling out burritos," he says.

Panhandling ploys such as asking passersby for bus money brought Baca as much as $45 in 20 minutes some days, though other days he made nothing, he says. A chronic alcoholic, Baca says he usually spent the money on alcohol. He estimates 95% of panhandlers spend donations on alcohol, drugs or cigarettes.

As an alternative to donating to either a meter or a pan handler, Donovan suggests having a conversation with the person.

"Then the person becomes real and is not just an object of annoyance you'd like to see removed from your daily commute," he says.

> "Homeless people face a myriad of issues that require specialized services. . . . If these services are cut, we anticipate a precipitous increase in homelessness."

Cutting Assistance for Homelessness Would Be Disastrous

Chicago Alliance to End Homelessness

Like their counterparts in agencies all across the country, state-funded social services providers in Illinois are grappling with devastating budget cuts and delayed payments as their state struggles to make ends meet and balance its budget. To understand the real-world impact that deep cuts would have on both programs and people, the Chicago Alliance to End Homelessness (CAEH) conducted a comprehensive survey of sixty-six social services agencies in the state. The following viewpoint details CAEH's findings and includes comments from care providers, who explain in their own words what budget cuts will mean for their agencies and the day-to-day lives of the clients they serve.

As you read, consider the following questions:

1. What do the authors say will happen if Illinois continues to sacrifice homeless and housing programs?

2. According to the authors, what have agencies been
forced to do because payments from the state are badly
delayed?

3. What do the authors say agencies would have to do if
homeless programs are cut substantially?

From February 22 to March 12, 2010, throughout the State
of Illinois, state-funded social service providers for people
who are homeless or at risk of homelessness and/or who need
affordable housing completed an online survey to document
the impact of the state budget crisis on their ability to serve
individuals and families. The results show that most providers
are struggling to stay afloat in the wake of dramatic budget
cuts, delayed state payments and the uncertainty of even more
drastic cuts in the future. This report outlines the survey results and captures the devastating impact of the budget crisis
on our efforts to end homelessness and ensure that all Illi-
noisans have safe, affordable housing.

The sixty-six agencies that completed the survey are
funded by line items that receive a combined $36.5 million in
state funding in the current fiscal year—line items that have
collectively seen a 23% decrease from previous high funding
levels.

While $36.5 million represents only a small portion of
state funding—less than 1% of the $4 billion in total General
Revenue Funding for the Illinois Department of Human Services (IDHS)—these programs are an integral component of
efforts to end homelessness and secure housing for our most
vulnerable citizens.

The harm caused by cuts to these programs are also troubling examples of the larger impact of cuts to human services

overall. For example, Governor Pat Quinn's FY11 [fiscal year 2011] budget proposal for the IDHS's Division of Mental Health includes cuts that could, according to IDHS, result in 4,000 people with severe mental illness losing their supervised or supported housing.

If Illinois continues to sacrifice homeless and housing programs, we will not only go backward in time, but we will also trigger an increase in homelessness.

The main messages from the survey are presented in the Key Findings section. Throughout this brief report, we also intersperse quotes from providers who responded to the survey to illustrate the key findings. At the end of the report, we present a longer list of statements from social service providers. Taken individually the impact of each statement is small compared to the scope of the overall crisis. Collectively, they make a significant point about the devastating implications of continued state budget cuts and delayed payments.

"This is what we are most afraid of. Homeless people face a myriad of issues that require specialized services. . . . If these services are cut, we anticipate a precipitous increase in homelessness."—*Ryan Dowd, Hesed House/Public Action to Deliver Shelter, Inc. (PADS), Aurora*

Key Findings

Agencies are already turning people in need of housing away due to state budget cuts. Sixty-one agencies turned away 1,292 people in January 2010 because of prior year state budget cuts, representing 9% of the 13,720 people they were able to serve. This does not include additional people who were turned away for issues not related to state budget cuts, such as lack of bed space.

Agencies are already owed a significant amount of money by the state and are taking on additional debt to manage the crisis. In total, 54 agencies are owed $10.2 million from the state in delayed payments, or about $189,000 per agency. The average delay in state payments is slightly less than 3 months, with delays as high as 9 months. Forty-seven agencies have been forced to take on an average of $44,000 in additional debt in order to stay afloat.

State-funded programs create jobs and provide matching funds for federal government resources. State funding for 61 agencies supports more than 1,600 jobs across Illinois. Forty-nine agencies are leveraging $47.7 million in federal funds every year that depend on a state match.

More budget cuts will result in fewer people receiving services and the loss of state-funded jobs. Based on the responses of 66 agencies, if homeless programs are cut substantially in the FY11 budget, 79% of agencies would have to reduce services and 74% of agencies would have to lay off staff. Forty-one percent of agencies would have to eliminate programs.

Integral Components Are Jeopardized

While $36.5 million represents only a small portion of state funding—less than 1% of the $4 billion in total General Revenue Funding for the Illinois Department of Human Services (IDHS)—these programs are an integral component of efforts to end homelessness and secure housing for our most vulnerable citizens. Total state General Revenue Funding for the Illinois Department of Human Services in FY10 is $4,036,884,000.

Governor Quinn released his FY11 budget proposal on March 10. He proposed over $2 billion in cuts, including $1.3 billion in education cuts. Elementary and secondary education could be slashed about 17%, overall, while state universities could be cut about 6%. Child care for working families could be cut by 12% and substance-abuse prevention services by 10%, and the proposal would drastically slash mental health services.

The budget also relies on significant short-term borrowing and continued delayed payment of state bills. Although not included in his formal proposal, Governor Quinn is advocating for a 1% increase in the income tax (from 3% to 4%) as a way to avoid the education cuts in his proposal.

The cuts to the four homeless service line items highlighted in this report could be even more significant than what is included in Governor Quinn's budget proposal depending on the final budget approved by the General Assembly, especially if the General Assembly does not support any revenue increases.

Program Descriptions

Emergency and Transitional Housing: Formerly called the Emergency Food and Shelter Program, this program provides immediate and comprehensive shelter services to homeless persons and persons at risk of becoming homeless. Shelter programs in Illinois consist primarily of overnight shelters and transitional housing, where people can stay up to two years.

Homeless Prevention Program: This program provides rental assistance, utility assistance, and supportive services directly related to the prevention of homelessness to eligible individuals and families who are in danger of eviction, foreclosure, or homelessness, or are currently homeless. The program is designed to stabilize individuals and families in their existing homes, shorten the amount of time that individuals and families stay in shelters, and assist individuals and families with securing affordable housing.

Homeless Youth Program: Services are for youth who are 21 years of age or younger who cannot return home and lack the housing and resources necessary to live independently. The purpose of the program is to provide services that help homeless youth transition to independent living and become self-sufficient. The program strives to meet the immediate survival needs (food, clothing, and shelter) of youth and assist them in becoming self-sufficient.

A History of State Budget Cuts for Homeless Programs

The current state budget crisis has reduced funding for the following four homeless service line items by $10.6 million or 23% between previous high funding levels and Illinois governor Pat Quinn's proposed FY11 [fiscal year 2011] budget. Dollar amounts represent thousands.

State Budget Line Item	Previous High Funding Level	High Funding Year	FY10 Funding	FY11 Proposed Funding	$ Change High/ FY11P	% Change High/ FY11P
Emergency and Transitional Housing	9,700.0	FY03	9,123.6	9,104.9	(595.1)	(6%)
Homeless Prevention Program	11,000.0	FY09	2,400.0	2,400.0	(8,600.0)	(78%)
Homeless Youth Program	4,747.7	FY08	3,622.0	3,259.8	(1,487.9)	(31%)
Supportive Housing Services	21,347.5	FY10	21,347.5	21,347.5	0.0	0.0%
Total	$46,747.5		$36,493.1	$36,112.2	($10,683.0)	(23%)

TAKEN FROM: Chicago Alliance to End Homelessness, "A Devastating Impact: How More Budget Cuts and Delayed Payments Will Increase Homelessness in Illinois," March 24, 2010.

Supportive Housing Services: Provides supportive services coupled with affordable housing to enable formerly homeless individuals and families, those in danger of becoming homeless, or persons with disabilities to be appropriately and cost-efficiently housed in the community. The program is designed to prevent people returning to or falling into homelessness. The supportive services enhance the ability of individuals to maintain their housing and increase their self-sufficiency. . . .

Statements from Providers

The numbers in this report tell one part of the story. Another part of the story comes from the statements of social service providers about the impact of the state budget crisis. Taken individually the impact of each statement is small compared to the scope of the overall crisis. Collectively, they make a significant point about the devastating implications of continued state budget cuts and delayed payments. [Comments received include the following:]

- We do not have the same level of Homelessness Prevention Funding available, so we end up serving less clients. . . .

- The greatest impact to clients has been the reduction in services due to the elimination in direct care staff, i.e. case worker and supervisors. . . .

- Clients have had less contact with staff due to cutting positions down to bare bones. We have not been able to provide the same intensity and quality of services to the people we serve.

- With the reduction in funding for the Homeless Prevention Funding, we may be able to serve half of the clients we served in our 2009 funding year. . . .

- The reduction in state homeless prevention dollars has directly decreased the number of families we are able to help stay out of or leave homelessness. This year we are only able to assist approximately 33 families compared to the 141 families we were able to help one year ago before the program suffered a 70% funding cut.

- Limited resources—accessibility to social workers, nurses, after school help, due to staff reductions. The number of students served varies from day to day. Those living in shelters move in and out. We have seen a drastic increase in homelessness especially those doubling up. Delay of funds—3 to 5 months depending upon the funding source. . . .

- With not having homeless prevention funds available we had to turn away clients' request for assistance. . . .

- We have had to pull from other resources to keep our program afloat and to pay the staff salaries. We will not be able to continue this for any length of time. . . .

- We had to close 3 units of family housing in June 2009, due to delays in payments and anticipated budget reductions. This reduced the number of families we could serve, and lengthened the wait for families to get into our program.

> *"Vendors can make hundreds of dollars a month or more with sales and tips, giving them a basic level of income that has helped some rent apartments and pay for expenses such as medicine and utilities."*

Buying Street Newspapers Helps Homeless People Help Themselves

Anne Paine

Homeless people in cities across the country are making money selling street newspapers that are largely written and produced by homeless individuals themselves. As Anne Paine, a reporter for the Tennessean, *explains in the following viewpoint, Nashville is one of the latest cities to have its very own street news publication. Homeless people pay a small amount for each paper and get to keep the profits when they sell them for $1 each. Homeless advocates say street publications help bring homeless people a sense of pride and purpose as well as the stability that comes with having a reliable income. Those vendors who stick with it, Paine writes, can make enough money to rent an apart-*

ment and pay for basic necessities. Paine talks to several street paper vendors about how selling the publication has helped them get back on their feet.

As you read, consider the following questions:

1. What honor was bestowed upon Nashville's *Contributor* street newspaper in the summer of 2009?

2. The author explains that street newspaper vendors must do what to sell the papers?

3. How can street newspaper vendors earn additional copies to sell for profit?

Hawking a monthly newspaper written by Nashville's homeless and formerly homeless may seem to offer an unlikely path to stability, especially at a time when media companies across the U.S. are suffering.

But for Jerry Andreasen, and his wife, Karren, both 65, selling copies of *The Contributor* at $1 a copy has helped them move from a tent by the river to renting a $100-a-week room in a North Nashville house. A carpenter and handyman, Jerry Andreasen had lost everything after he had a heart attack.

"You don't start out with no mansion," he said, as he walked around the couple's shared room jammed with newly acquired tools, many donated. "This here tickles us to death."

The couple are part of a national movement that is changing the discussion about street people by making them micro-businessmen and putting a personal face on poverty.

Vendors can make hundreds of dollars a month or more with sales and tips, giving them a basic level of income that has helped some rent apartments and pay for expenses such as medicine and utilities.

Andy Freeze, executive director of the North American Street Newspaper Association, said circulation is rising among the papers. There are about 25 street newspapers in 10 cities in the U.S. and Canada.

In its first two months of publication in 2007, Nashville's *Contributor* sold about 600 copies. By August of this year [2009], 4,500 had been distributed, and sales have been brisk enough that the 6,000-copy run of its September issue could sell out. Nashville's paper this summer won an award for a piece by Michael "Pontiac" Cooke about making the transition from a tent city to a subsidized apartment.

Freeze said Seattle's *Real Change News* has reached a circulation of 70,000 a month, and the *Denver Voice* jumped from 9,800 a year ago to about 15,000.

"It isn't the easiest job, but persistence and patience are very important as well as sales skills," Freeze said. "The best vendors are persistent, patient and polite."

Taking Positive Steps

Graphic designer and photographer Tasha French and artist Tom Wills, who started *The Contributor*, have trained more than 230 vendors in Nashville.

Vendors must sign a code of conduct that requires sobriety while working, respect toward all, staying off private property and wearing an identification badge. The vendors start out with 15 free papers to sell for a dollar plus any tips, and can buy additional copies for 25 cents.

That 25 cents covers the printing of the 16-page tabloid and extras such as badges, bags to carry papers and an intern who edits articles. Costs run about $950 a month, Wills said.

Attending vendor meetings at Downtown Presbyterian Church, site of the paper's office, and writing articles are among the activities that can earn individuals additional free copies.

The articles and photographs give a window into the lives of some of the sellers and others like them.

Pieces in recent *Contributor* issues looked at personal stories of addiction and redemption, the difficulty of trying to get by on minimum wage, why some people hate the homeless, urban gardens, a bicycle repair workshop for public housing youth, and a review of the Tomato Art Festival in East Nashville. There's even a locally written "Hoboscope" column that offers amateur astrology readings.

Some don't stay with the job because of the discipline it takes, but about 55 vendors are selling this month [September 2009] with several regulars who have become familiar to and trusted by many downtown workers and police officers, said French, the paper's director, who is a volunteer.

Tom Turner, president and CEO [chief executive officer] of the Nashville Downtown Partnership, a business-oriented group that wants to keep aggressive panhandlers and drunks away from the area, said he appreciates what *The Contributor* is doing for the homeless population.

"If you have a group of courteous people trying to better their position, I think it's good for them and good for the community," Turner said. "For a lot of people, quality of life can start with a job. Anything that provides a part of the solution is a step in the right direction."

Turner gave *The Contributor* an endorsement: He reads parts of the paper.

"Some of it's very interesting, and some is very entertaining," he said. "You can learn a little about what's going on."

Attention for the Homeless Cause

Leaving Downtown Presbyterian Church last week [in September 2009], Tony Angello looked like a tourist, with sunglasses perched atop his bald head, tidy jeans and a bright Hawaiian shirt. But the stack of newspapers under his arm told a different story. He and his wife, Quita Thornton, were on their way to sell *The Contributor*.

Until two weeks ago, the couple were spending $40 to $50 a night on motel rooms.

"It was important we make those (newspaper) sales or we slept in the street," Angello said.

Street Newspapers in the United States and Canada

The Amplifier, Knoxville, Tennessee

Community Connections, Los Angeles, California

The Contributor, Nashville, Tennessee

Denver Dialogue, Denver, Colorado

Edmonton Street News, Edmonton, Alberta

Forgotten Voice, Las Vegas, Nevada

Groundcover News, Ann Arbor, Michigan

Heartland News, Omaha, Nebraska

Homeless Image, St. Petersburg, Florida

L'Itineraire, Montreal, Quebec

Megaphone, Vancouver, British Columbia

One Step Away, Philadelphia, Pennsylvania

Real Change, Seattle, Washington

Salt Lake Street News, Salt Lake City, Utah

Spare Change News, Cambridge, Massachusetts

Street Feat Halifax, Nova Scotia

Street Beat, Honolulu, Hawaii

Street Pulse, Madison, Wisconsin

Street Roots, Portland, Oregon

Street Sights, Pawtucket, Rhode Island

Street Sense, Washington, D.C.

Street Sheet, Winnipeg, Manitoba

Street Zine, Dallas, Texas

Streetvibes, Cincinnati, Ohio

StreetWise, Chicago, Illinois

What's Up Magazine St. Louis, Missouri

Compiled by editor using information from the North American Street Newspaper Association. www.nasna.org.

They decided to buy a tent and now sleep in an isolated, wooded area so they can save for an apartment. . . .

Office worker Chantay Shye threw her arms around vendor Debbie Overstreet outside the Arcade and gave her $3. She said she worries when she doesn't see Overstreet selling the paper.

"Some of them are some good people," Shye said, grinning at Overstreet. "I don't know how it feels to be homeless. I don't want to know. I help people when I can."

Overstreet, 49, smiling but with a serious look in her eyes, called out as people passed: "September edition is out. Want to buy a paper to help the homeless and formerly homeless?"

"I'm almost at the same level," one middle-age man said with a nod as he passed.

"Have a blessed day," she said.

Overstreet, looking like somebody's big sister with blond ponytail and clean white tennis shoes, said she was disabled in a car wreck. When her husband divorced her and didn't pay alimony, she lost everything.

She has managed to get into federally subsidized housing, but needs money from paper sales for basic things such as toiletries, telephone service and washing clothes.

"This is like my own business," she said.

A man who looked to be in his 30s stopped to ask her over the roar of a passing bus how he could get a job selling the paper. He was the third person that day to ask, she said.

Periodical and Internet Sources Bibliography

The following articles have been selected to supplement the diverse views presented in this chapter.

Mike Aldax	"City's Homeless Programs Touted," *San Francisco Examiner*, October 28, 2009. www.sfexaminer.com.
Julie Bosman	"City Aids Homeless with One-Way Tickets Home," *New York Times*, July 28, 2009. www.nytimes.com.
Henri E. Cauvin	"Administration Broadens Effort to Fight Homelessness," *Washington Post*, June 23, 2010. www.washingtonpost.com.
Ronny Dory	"Cities Install Donation Meters for the Homeless—'Giving Meters' Support Programs, Reduce Panhandling," *Epoch Times*, September 16, 2010. www.theepochtimes.com.
Pam Fessler	"Ending Homelessness: A Model That Just Might Work," National Public Radio, March 7, 2011. www.npr.org.
David Jefferson	"Spare Change's Most Insidious Myths," *Spare Change News* (Boston), March 11, 2010. http://sparechangenews.net.
Ian Merrifield	"The Ten-Year Plan," *Harvard Political Review*, May 24, 2009. http://hpronline.org.
Jon Morgenstern	"'Housing First' and Helping the Homeless," *Los Angeles Times*, August 15, 2010. www.latimes.com.
National Coalition for the Homeless and The National Law Center on Homelessness & Poverty	"A Place at the Table: Prohibitions on Sharing Food with People Experiencing Homelessness," NCH/NLCHP, July 2010.

For Further Discussion

Chapter 1

1. The authors in this chapter discuss various groups of people who are particularly affected by homelessness. Are there any characteristics that these groups share? In what ways might they be similar?

2. Youth who are LGBT (lesbian, gay, bisexual, and transgender) or who are in the foster care system are especially vulnerable to becoming homeless. What kinds of special issues might a young person who is homeless face, as opposed to someone who is older and of legal age?

3. According to the viewpoints in this chapter, how is the homeless population different than it was twenty years ago?

Chapter 2

1. Of all the various factors that contribute to homelessness, which do you think plays the biggest role for people who are chronically homeless? Why?

2. What kinds of other events or circumstances, not discussed in this chapter, do you think might lead a person to become homeless?

Chapter 3

1. Do you think homeless people should be given free housing without first requiring them to get treatment for mental health problems or alcohol and drug addictions? Why or why not?

2. What are the pros and cons of citing homeless people for violating quality-of-life laws, such as panhandling or urinating in public?

3. What does it say about American priorities that housing is considered a human right by much of the world but not in the United States?

Chapter 4

1. The federal government's *Opening Doors: Federal Strategic Plan to Prevent and End Homelessness* is the most ambitious effort of its kind. Do you think the program will meet its goals of ending homelessness among veterans in five years and ending homelessness for families, youth, and children in ten years? Why or why not? What obstacles might this plan face?

2. Does your city have a street newspaper that homeless people can sell to earn money? If so, and you have never read one, why not?

3. Can you think of an idea of your own that might help reduce homelessness?

Organizations to Contact

The editors have compiled the following list of organizations concerned with the issues debated in this book. The descriptions are derived from materials provided by the organizations. All have publications or information available for interested readers. The list was compiled on the date of publication of the present volume; names, addresses, phone and fax numbers, and e-mail and Internet addresses may change. Be aware that many organizations take several weeks or longer to respond to inquiries, so allow as much time as possible.

AARP

601 E Street NW, Washington, DC 20049
(888) OUR-AARP
e-mail: member@aarp.org
website: www.aarp.org

AARP, formerly known as the American Association of Retired Persons, is the country's largest membership organization for senior citizens. AARP publishes *AARP The Magazine* and the *AARP Bulletin* newsletter. Issue statements and congressional testimony can be found on the AARP's website, and its magazine and newsletter content is archived there as well. Recently archived articles related to homelessness include "Homeless Veterans No More—Nonprofit 'Soldier On' Provides Affordable Housing, Support and Job Training," "Older Low-Income Workers on the Brink of Homelessness," and "No Place to Call Home: Older Homeless in the U.S."

American Civil Liberties Union (ACLU)

125 Broad Street, 18th Floor, New York, NY 10004
(212) 549-2500
e-mail: info@aclu.org
website: www.aclu.org

Through activism in courts, legislatures, and communities nationwide, the American Civil Liberties Union (ACLU) works to defend and preserve the individual rights and liberties that the Constitution and laws of the United States guarantee everyone. The ACLU's website has an extensive collection of reports, briefings, and news updates related to homelessness and the rights of homeless individuals. Reports available on the website include "Fair Housing for Battered Women: Preventing Homelessness Through Civil Rights Law" and "HIV and Homeless Shelters: Policy and Practice."

Cato Institute
1000 Massachusetts Avenue NW
Washington, DC   20001-5403
(202) 842-0200 • fax: (202) 842-3490
website: www.cato.org

The Cato Institute is a public policy research foundation dedicated to limiting the role of government, protecting individual liberties, and promoting free markets. The institute commissions a variety of publications including books, monographs, briefing papers, and other studies. Among its publications are the quarterly magazine *Regulation* and the bimonthly *Cato Policy Report*. It offers an extensive selection of materials online, including articles such as "Homeless Scare Numbers," "Housing Policy in New York: Myth and Reality," and "ID Requirements and the Indigent."

Homelessness Resource Center
SAMHSA's Health Information Network
Rockville, MD   20847-2345
(877) SAMHSA-7 • fax: (240) 221-4292
e-mail: generalinquiry@center4si.com
website: homeless.samhsa.gov

The Homelessness Resource Center is a program of the US Department of Health and Human Services (HHS) Substance Abuse and Mental Health Services Administration (SAMHSA), Center for Mental Health Services. The center is an interactive

community of providers, consumers, policy makers, researchers, and public agencies at the federal, state, and local levels.
The organization's mission is to improve the lives of people
affected by homelessness who have mental health conditions,
substance use issues, and histories of trauma. The center seeks
to prevent and end homelessness through training and technical assistance, publications and materials, online learning opportunities, and networking and collaboration. Its website
maintains an extensive library of homeless-related materials,
including the US Department of Housing and Urban
Development's *2010 Annual Homeless Assessment Report to
Congress*; the book *Homelessness, Housing and Mental Illness*;
the interview "Youth Homelessness"; and the article "Shining
Spotlight on Needs of the Homeless," along with numerous
reports from the National Coalition for the Homeless and
other agencies that serve the homeless.

Homes for the Homeless (HFH)

50 Cooper Square, 4th Floor, New York, NY   10003
(212) 529-5252 • fax: (212) 529-7698
e-mail: info@hfhnyc.org
website: www.hfhnyc.org

Homes for the Homeless (HFH) works to reduce homelessness by providing families with the education and training
they need to build independent lives. Participating families are
housed in one of four residential educational training centers
throughout New York, where they learn job, literacy, and
parenting skills. Participants are also counseled on substance
abuse and domestic violence. HFH publishes a monthly newsletter and has authored numerous reports, which are available
on its website. Titles include "Homelessness: The Foster Care
Connection," "The New Poverty: A Generation of Homeless
Families," "An American Family Myth: Every Child at Risk,"
and "Job Readiness: Crossing the Threshold from Homelessness to Employment."

National Alliance to End Homelessness (NAEH)

1518 K Street NW, Suite 410, Washington, DC   20005
(202) 638-1526 • fax: (202) 638-4664
e-mail: naeh@naeh.org
website: www.endhomelessness.org

The National Alliance to End Homelessness (NAEH) is a nonpartisan organization committed to preventing and ending homelessness in the United States. The organization develops policy solutions that help homeless individuals and families make positive changes in their lives, and it provides research to policy makers and elected officials to inform policy debates. The organization provides fact sheets, reports, presentations, briefs, and case studies on its website, including the publications "A Progress Report on the Federal Strategic Plan to Prevent and End Homelessness," "State of Homelessness in America 2011," and "Geography of Homelessness."

National Alliance on Mental Illness (NAMI)

3803 N. Fairfax Drive, Suite 100, Arlington, VA   22203
(703) 524-7600 • fax: (703) 524-9094
website: www.nami.org

The National Alliance on Mental Illness (NAMI) is the nation's largest grassroots mental health advocacy organization, and its mission is to eradicate mental illnesses and improve the quality of life of those affected by such diseases. NAMI publishes the monthly *Advocate* magazine, and its website offers an extensive collection of congressional testimony and legislative updates related to mental health, including mental health and homelessness. Publications available on its website include "'Housing First' Approach Benefits Both Consumers and Law Enforcement" and "The High Costs of Cutting Mental Health: Homelessness."

National Coalition for the Homeless (NCH)

2201 P Street NW, Washington, DC   20037
(202) 462-4822 • fax: (202) 462-4823

c-mail: info@nationalhomcless.org
website: www.nationalhomeless.org

The National Coalition for the Homeless (NCH) is a national network of people who are currently experiencing or who have experienced homelessness, activists and advocates, community-based and faith-based service providers, and others committed to ending homelessness. The NCH website offers a variety of reports, news items, and announcements about homeless issues, as well as the blog *Bring America Home*. Among the reports and papers available on the site are "A Place at the Table: Prohibitions on Sharing Food with People Experiencing Homelessness" and "Hate Crimes Against the Homeless: America's Growing Tide of Violence."

National Coalition for Homeless Veterans (NCHV)
333½ Pennsylvania Avenue SE
Washington, DC   20003-1148
(800) VET-HELP • fax (202) 546-2063
e-mail: info@nchv.org
website: www.nchv.org

The National Coalition for Homeless Veterans (NCHV) is a nonprofit organization that operates as a resource and technical assistance center for a national network of agencies that provide emergency and supportive housing, food, health services, job training and placement assistance, legal aid, and case management support for hundreds of thousands of homeless veterans each year. NCHV works to end homelessness among veterans by shaping public policy, promoting collaboration, and building the capacity of service providers. NCHV publishes information to provide assistance to community and faith-based organizations, government agencies, corporate partners, and the homeless veterans they serve. NCHV publishes a monthly e-newsletter and resources such as the "Homeless Veterans Assistance Guide" and the fact sheet "How to Advocate for a Homeless Veteran." The website also includes a collection of reports and resources that specifically pertain to female veterans.

National Gay and Lesbian Task Force

1325 Massachusetts Avenue NW, Suite 600
Washington, DC 20005
(202) 393-5177 • fax: (202) 393-2241
e-mail: info@thetaskforce.org
website: www.thetaskforce.org

The National Gay and Lesbian Task Force works to build the grassroots power of the lesbian, gay, bisexual, and transgender (LGBT) community by training activists and helping to strengthen their organizational capacity. The group's Policy Institute is the premier think tank of the LGBT movement, and its website features reports, legislative updates, and news items about homelessness in the LGBT community, including reports on youth homelessness in various cities nationwide.

National Health Care for the Homeless Council (NHCHC)

PO Box 60427, Nashville, TN 37206-0427
(615) 226-2292 • fax: (615) 226-1656
website: www.nhchc.org

The National Health Care for the Homeless Council (NHCHC) works closely with other service providers and advocates toward the elimination of homelessness. It organizes an annual policy symposium that examines the impact of public policies on homeless people, and it contributes to various conferences, meetings, and studies regarding health and homelessness each year. The group publishes the monthly *Healing Hands* newsletter, and its website offers a variety of policy statements and research reports related to homelessness. Publications available from the website include the 2011 "Data Resource Guide: Learning About Homelessness and Health in Your Community" and the report *Providing Treatment for Homeless Persons with Substance Use Disorders: Six Case Studies.*

National Law Center on Homelessness & Poverty (NLCHP)

1411 K Street NW, Suite 1400, Washington, DC 20005
(202) 638-2535 • fax: (202) 628-2737
website: www.nlchp.org

The National Law Center on Homelessness & Poverty (NLCHP) advocates to protect the rights of homeless people and to implement solutions to end homelessness in America. To achieve its mission, the center pursues three main strategies: impact litigation, policy advocacy, and public education. The NLCHP's website offers information about homelessness and poverty and the center's various programs and activities. The NLCHP posts timely action alerts and a monthly newsletter, which is archived on its website.

National Runaway Switchboard (NRS)
3080 N. Lincoln Avenue, Chicago, IL 60657
(800) RUN-AWAY • fax: (773) 929-5150
website: www.1800runaway.org

The National Runaway Switchboard (NRS) operates a confidential hotline for runaway youth, teens in crisis, and concerned friends and family members. All services are free and available twenty-four hours every day. NRS services include crisis intervention; message relay between runaways and their parent/legal guardian; referrals and conference to community-based resources, such as counseling, support groups, alternative housing, and health care; Home Free program in partnership with Greyhound Lines, Inc., to help runaways return home to their families; education and outreach services; and free NRS promotional materials for distribution at community events, school assemblies, and health fairs.

**National Student Campaign Against Hunger
and Homelessness (NSCAHH)**
328 S. Jefferson Street, Suite 620, Chicago, IL 60661
(312) 544-4436 x204 • fax: (312) 275-7150
e-mail: info@studentsagainsthunger.org
website: www.studentsagainsthunger.org/

The National Student Campaign Against Hunger and Homelessness (NSCAHH) works with coalitions of students and community members across the country to end hunger and homelessness through education, service, and action. The

NSCAHH is the largest student network fighting hunger and homelessness in the country, with more than six hundred participating campuses in forty-five states. The campaign trains students to improve or create service programs to meet the needs of the hungry and homeless in their communities. It also holds workshops and conferences to educate people about the antipoverty movement. Its website offers resources such as an interactive map of poverty in the United States, the fact sheets "Homelessness in America" and "Overview of World Hunger," the Urban Institute report *Homelessness: Programs and the People They Serve*, and a recommended reading list for those interested in issues related to hunger and homelessness.

North American Street Newspaper Association (NASNA)
NASNA c/o The Contributor, Nashville, TN   37219
e-mail: info@nasna.org
website: www.nasna.org

The North American Street Newspaper Association (NASNA) is a nonprofit trade association of street newspapers throughout North America. NASNA has twenty-three member papers in the United States and eight in Canada. Its mission is to support and cultivate an effective, self-sustaining street newspaper network that promotes power and opportunity for people living in poverty. The organization works with more than eighteen hundred homeless individuals who sell more than three hundred thousand newspapers each month. NASNA publishes a monthly newsletter, and its website features information about the street paper movement, personal stories of street paper vendors, and instructions on how to start a new street publication. The website also includes a comprehensive list of all known street newspapers in the United States and Canada.

United States Conference of Mayors Task Force on Hunger and Homelessness
1620 Eye Street NW, Washington, DC   20006
(202) 293-7330 • fax: (202) 293-2352

e-mail: info@usmayors.org
website: http://usmayors.org

Created in 1932, the United States Conference of Mayors (USCM) is the official nonpartisan organization of cities with populations of thirty thousand or more. There are 1,192 such cities in the country today. Each city is represented in the conference by its chief elected official, the mayor. The USCM Task Force on Hunger and Homelessness studies trends in hunger, homelessness, and community programs that address homelessness and hunger in US cities. It publishes an annual report on hunger and homelessness. The current and previous years' reports are available on its website.

United States Interagency Council on Homelessness (USICH)

Federal Center SW, 409 Third Street SW, Suite 310
Washington, DC   20024
(202) 708-4663 • fax: (202) 708-1216
e-mail: usich@usich.gov
website: www.usich.gov

The United States Interagency Council on Homelessness (USICH) is composed of nineteen cabinet secretaries and agency heads, plus staff. The council reviews, monitors, evaluates, and recommends improvements in federal homeless assistance programs. It is responsible for creating the federal government's ten-year strategic plan to end homelessness, known as *Opening Doors: The Federal Strategic Plan to Prevent and End Homelessness,* which is available in its entirety on the council's website. The council publishes the newsletter *Council Communiqué* and its website includes an extensive collection of reports and fact sheets about homelessness.

Bibliography of Books

Rebeca Antoine — *Voices Rising: Stories from the Katrina Narrative Project*. New Orleans: University of New Orleans Press, 2009.

Milton Argeriou and Dennis McCarty, eds. — *Treating Alcoholism and Drug Abuse Among Homeless Men and Women: Nine Community Demonstration Grants*. New York: Haworth Press, 1990.

Claire J. Baker and Mary Rudge — *Poems from Street Spirit: Justice News and Homeless Blues*. Bloomington, IN: Xlibris Corporation, 2005.

Jim Baumohl, ed. — *Homelessness in America*. Phoenix, AZ: Oryx Press, 1996.

Greg Berman and John Feinblatt — *Good Courts: The Case for Problem-Solving Justice*. New York: New Press, 2005.

Joel Blau — *The Visible Poor: Homelessness in the United States*. New York: Oxford University Press, 1992.

Lynn Blodgett — *Finding Grace: The Face of America's Homeless*. San Rafael, CA: Earth Aware Editions, 2007.

Rachel G. Bratt, Michael E. Stone, and Chester Hartman, eds. — *A Right to Housing: Foundation for a New Social Agenda*. Philadelphia: Temple University Press, 2006.

C.T. Lawrence Butler and Keith McHenry	*Food Not Bombs.* Tucson, AZ: See Sharp Press, 2000.
Tim Connelly	*Home Without a Home.* Lulu.com, 2008.
Kevin Cwayna	*Knowing Where the Fountains Are: Stories and Stark Realities of Homeless Youth.* Minneapolis: Fairview Press, 1996.
Timothy E. Donohue	*In the Open: Diary of a Homeless Alcoholic.* Chicago: University of Chicago Press, 1996.
Ingrid Gould Ellen and Brendan O'Flaherty, eds.	*How to House the Homeless.* New York: Russell Sage Foundation, 2010.
Marni Finkelstein	*With No Direction Home: Homeless Youth on the Road and in the Streets.* Belmont, CA: Thomson/Wadsworth, 2005.
Teresa Gowan	*Hobos, Hustlers, and Backsliders: Homeless in San Francisco.* Minneapolis: University of Minnesota Press, 2010.
Jed Horne	*Breach of Faith: Hurricane Katrina and the Near Death of a Great American City.* New York: Random House, 2008.
Christopher Jencks	*The Homeless.* Cambridge, MA: Harvard University Press, 1994.

Jonathan Kozol   *Rachel and Her Children: Homeless Families in America.* New York: Three Rivers Press, 2006.

Kenneth L. Kusmer   *Down & Out, On the Road: The Homeless in American History.* New York: Oxford University Press, 2002.

David Levinson, ed.   *Encyclopedia of Homelessness.* Thousand Oaks, CA: Sage Publications, 2004.

David Levinson and Marcy Ross, eds.   *Homelessness Handbook.* Great Barrington, MA: Berkshire Publishing Group, 2007.

Jay S. Levy   *Homeless Narratives & Pretreatment Pathways: From Words to Housing.* Ann Arbor, MI: Loving Healing Press, 2010.

Elliot Liebow   *Tell Them Who I Am: The Lives of Homeless Women.* New York: Free Press, 1993.

Sassafras Lowrey, ed.   *Kicked Out.* Ypsilanti, MI: Homofactus Press, 2010.

Anthony Marcus   *Where Have All the Homeless Gone?: The Making and Unmaking of a Crisis.* New York: Berghahn Books, 2005.

Keith McHenry   *Cooking for Peace: Cultivating Community, Reaping Revolution, Transforming the World with Food Not Bombs.* El Prado, NM: Levine Mesa Press, 2011.

Jessica P. Morrell *Voices from the Street: Truths about Homelessness from Sisters of the Road.* Portland, OR: Gray Sunshine, 2007.

Matthew O'Brien *Beneath the Neon: Life and Death in the Tunnels of Las Vegas.* Las Vegas: Huntington Press, 2007.

Joel John Roberts *How to Increase Homelessness: Real Solutions to the Absurdity of Homelessness in America.* Bend, OR: Loyal Publishing, 2004.

Paul A. Rollinson and John T. Pardeck *Homelessness in Rural America: Policy and Practice.* New York: Haworth Press, 2006.

Peter H. Rossi *Down and Out in America: The Origins of Homelessness.* Chicago: University of Chicago Press, 1991.

Russell K. Schutt and Stephen M. Goldfinger *Homelessness, Housing, and Mental Illness.* Cambridge, MA: Harvard University Press, 2011.

Stephen B. Seager *Street Crazy: America's Mental Health Tragedy.* Redondo Beach, CA: Westcom Press, 2000.

Scott Seider *Shelter: Where Harvard Meets the Homeless.* New York: Continuum, 2010.

Jennifer Toth *The Mole People: Life in the Tunnels Beneath New York City.* Chicago: Chicago Review Press, 1995.

Yvonne Vissing — *Out of Sight, Out of Mind: Homeless Children and Families in Small-Town America*. Lexington: University Press of Kentucky, 1996.

Alex S. Vitale — *City of Disorder: How the Quality of Life Campaign Transformed New York Politics*. New York: New York University Press, 2008.

Tom Waits and Michael O'Brien — *Hard Ground*. Austin: University of Texas Press, 2011.

Jean Calterone Williams — *"A Roof over My Head": Homeless Women and the Shelter Industry*. Boulder: University Press of Colorado, 2003.

James D. Wright — *Address Unknown: The Homeless in America*. New Brunswick, NJ: AldineTransaction, 2009.

Michael Yankoski — *My 30 Days Under the Overpass: Not Your Ordinary Devotional*. Sisters, OR: Multnomah Books, 2006.

Michael Yankoski — *Under the Overpass: A Journey of Faith on the Streets of America*. Sisters, OR: Multnomah Books, 2005.

Index